Enameling

PRINCIPLES AND PRACTICE

by Kenneth F. Bates

CLEVELAND AND NEW YORK

THE WORLD PUBLISHING COMPANY

Published by
THE WORLD PUBLISHING COMPANY

First Edition

GA 451

Copyright 1951 by The World Publishing Company
All rights reserved No part of this book may be reproduced in any form without written permission from the publisher, except for brief passages included in a review appearing in a newspaper or magazine. Manufactured in the United States of America

Design and Typography by
Joseph Trautwein

CONTENTS

FOREWORD   *page*   13

INTRODUCTION   17

I

A BRIEF HISTORY OF ENAMELING: Greek enamels · Celtic enamels · Byzantine enamels · German enamels · French enamels · Enameled portraits · English enamels · Russian enamels · Chinese and Japanese enamels · English revival in 1864 · Viennese school · Enameling in America   *page*   21

II

HOW ENAMELS ARE COMPOUNDED AND ENAMELING TOOLS AND MATERIALS Types of enamels · Silica · Oxide of lead · Borax · Potash and soda · Oxides of metal · Materials · Kilns · Tools · Gum tragacanth   *page*   39

III

MAKING THE FIRST PIECE OF ENAMEL: Shaping the copper · Trimming · Cleaning · Acid bath · Alkalizing · Washing the enamel · Applying the counterenamel · Firing the enamel · Tracing the design · Spatula method · Dusting method · Deep bowls · Warping · Blowtorch firing   *page*   49

IV

TESTING THE COLORS, THE USE OF METAL FOILS AND THE INDIVIDUAL PALETTE. Opaque tests · Metal foils · Transparent tests on copper · Transparent tests on pure silver · Enameling on sterling silver · Test for melting point · Palette   *page*   74

CONTENTS

V

CHARACTERISTICS OF CERTAIN ENAMELS. Black · White · Gray · Flux · Blue · Green Brown · Red · Purple Chartreuse · Yellow · Ivory *page* 83

VI

MAKING LIMOGES ENAMELS: Preparing the plaque · Counterenameling the plaque Designing the plaque · Transferring the design First coat of enamel · Paillons for plaque · Grisaille enameling Detail painting · Metallic lusters *page* 92

VII

MAKING CLOISONNÉ ENAMELS BY THE OLDER TECHNIQUE AND A MODERN VERSION. Forming panels · Cleaning the gold · Wire for cloisonné · Soldering cloisonné wires · Applying the enamel · Firing cloisonné · Stoning process · Shorter cloisonné method *page* 109

VIII

MAKING CHAMPLEVÉ, *PLIQUE-Á-JOUR*, *BASSE-TAILLE* AND OTHER TYPES OF ENAMELS: Design for champlevé · Plating · Preparing the copper · Etching with acid · Enamels for champlevé · Buffing and polishing ·*Plique-à-jour* process · *Plique-à-jour* on copper plate · *Plique-à-jour* on mica · *Plique-à-jour* by capillary attraction · Applying the enamel · *Basse-taille* process · Grisaille process · *En résille* process *page* 125

IX

DESIGN FOR ENAMELING AND THE UNDERSTANDING AND FEELING FOR THE MEDIUM OF ENAMELING. Scale · Vibration · Edges · Stress · Subject matter *page* 141

LIST OF ILLUSTRATIONS
X

EXPERIMENTS, SUGGESTIONS FOR NEW USES OF ENAMEL AND EARNING A LIVING BY ENAMELING· EXPERIMENT 1–Enameled jewels · EXPERIMENT 2–Gas flame colorations · EXPERIMENT 3–Enameling over fire glaze EXPERIMENT 4–Overglaze shading · EXPERIMENT 5–The thin enameled line · EXPERIMENT 6–The embossed line · EXPERIMENT 7–Sgraffito technique · EXPERIMENT 8–Enameling on brass · EXPERIMENT 9–Textures with glass
page 160

APPENDIX
Materials for Enameling and Where to Buy Them · Contemporary American Enamelists · Tables of Information Useful to the Enamelist · Where to Find Information on How to Color Copper *page* 189

GLOSSARY *page* 199

BIBLIOGRAPHY *page* 203

INDEX *page* 204

LIST OF ILLUSTRATIONS

Gold and ebony box with cloisonné enamel (KENNETH F. BATES) *Frontispiece*

HISTORY OF ENAMELING

1	*Christ,* German medallion	*page* 22
2	Cover of a reliquary, Byzantine	23
3	Two champlevé plaques, French	25
4	*The Baptism and the Crucifixion*	26
5	Two crosses and portable altar from Guelph Treasure	27
6	Flabellum, champlevé	28

LIST OF ILLUSTRATIONS

7	*Portrait of François de Cleves* (LÉONARD LIMOUSIN)	page 30
8	*The Month of May* (PIERRE REYMOND)	31
9	*Mirror—Juno,* French Limoges	32
10	Enameled needlecase, English	33
11	Enameled workbox, English	33
12	Japanese cloisonné	35

ENAMELING TOOLS AND MATERIALS

13	Materials for the beginner in enameling	44
14	Small kiln	46
15	Homemade kiln	47
16	Three tools for enameling	48

MAKING THE FIRST PIECE OF ENAMEL

17	Simple concave shapes for first tray	50
18	Hammering in a stake tree	51
19	Planishing the tray	51
20	Trimming the tray	52
21	Removal of grease	53
22	Acid solution	53
23	Polishing the tray	54
24	Alkalizing the tray	55
25-26	Washing the enamel	56, 57
27	Counterenamel, dusting method	58
28	Gum tragacanth solution	59
29	Methods of placing tray in the kiln	60
30	Tongs	61
31	Swabbing tray with acid	64
32	Tracing the design	64
33	Spatular method	65
34	Stilts and stands for firing	66
35	*Bird of Paradise Flower* (KENNETH F. BATES)	67
36-37	Dusting method	68, 69
38	*Strelitzia* (KENNETH F. BATES)	70
39	*The Royal Family* (KENNETH F. BATES)	between 64, 65

LIST OF ILLUSTRATIONS

39	*Fruits of My Orchard* (KENNETH F. BATES)	*between* 64, 65
39	*Hibiscus Flower* (KENNETH F BATES)	70, 71
39	*Experiment 9B* (KENNETH F BATES)	70, 71
40	Enameling on deep bowls	*page* 71
41	Warping	72
42	Miniature muffled furnace	73

TESTING THE COLORS

43	Transparent and opaque enamel tests	75
44	Punch for silver paillons	77
45	Burnishing silver paillons	78
46	Glass brush for finishing silver	80

CHARACTERISTICS OF CERTAIN ENAMELS

47	*Cineraries* (KENNETH F BATES)	86
47A	*Reliquary*, Flemish champlevé	86
47A	*Ballet of Fishes* (KENNETH F. BATES)	86

MAKING LIMOGES ENAMELS

48	*Triptych—Crucifixion, St John and St Catharine*, Limoges	93
49	*Ewer—Nude Men in Combat* (PIERRE REYMOND)	94
50	Chasing hammer for forming Limoges panel	95
51	Edges of enamel plaque	95
52	Shaping the plaque	96
53	Shaping a circular plaque	96
54	Counterenamel and front enamel	98
55	Shapes of silver paillons	101
56	*Staff of Life* (KENNETH F. BATES)	103
57	*Argument in a Limoges Market Place* (KENNETH F. BATES)	105
58	*Inception of Spring* (KENNETH F. BATES)	106
59	*Portrait of a Lady* (LÉONARD LIMOUSIN)	107
60	*The Bird Watch* (KENNETH F. BATES)	108

MAKING CLOISONNÉ ENAMELS

61	Gold cloisonné medallion, Byzantine	110
62	Cloisonné designs	110
63-64	Soldering cloisonné wires	111, 114

LIST OF ILLUSTRATIONS

65	Grinding the enamel	page 115
66	Cloisonné enameling	116
67	Stoning process	117
68	*The Herd Boy on His Water Buffalo,* cloisonné	118
69	Cloisonné wires left unsoldered	119
70	Counterenameling	120
71	Bending cloisonné wire into shape	121
72	Enamels and surface of panel	122
73	First layer of enamel	122
74	Gold and silver foil	123
75	Forming a bezel	124
76	Completed cloisonné panel	124

MAKING CHAMPLEVÉ, PLIQUE-À-JOUR, BASSE-TAILLE AND OTHER ENAMELS

77	*Eucharistic Dove,* champlevé	126
78	Design for champlevé	127
79	Dispersing bubbles from metal surface	128
80	Stoning champlevé	130
81	*Vigil Light* (KENNETH F BATES)	131
82	Design for *plique-à-jour*	132
83	Firing *plique-à-jour* on mica	133
84	Firing *plique-à-jour* by capillary attraction	134
85	*Plique-à-jour* on copper window screening	135
86	French reliquary, *basse-taille*	135
87	Tools for carving in *basse-taille*	136
88	*A Pagan Sacrifice* (JEAN POILLEVÉ)	137
89	Vanity mirror, *en résille*	139

DESIGN FOR ENAMELING

90	Creating a design from free brush strokes	142
91	*Kilarney, Ontario* (KENNETH F. BATES)	145
92	*Gloxinias* (KENNETH F. BATES)	146
93	Diagram of *Kilarney, Ontario*	148
94	*Jungle Rhythms* (KENNETH F. BATES)	149

LIST OF ILLUSTRATIONS

95	Diagram of *Jungle Rhythms*	page 149
96	*Delineation* (KENNETH F. BATES)	151
97	*Sporangia* (KENNETH F. BATES)	152
98	*The Chase* (KENNETH F. BATES)	152
99	*Spring Comes in My Window* (KENNETH F. BATES)	153
100	*Flower Arrangement* (KENNETH F. BATES)	154
101	*My Trip to Pittsburgh* (KENNETH F BATES)	154
102	*Stations of the Cross* (KENNETH F. BATES)	155
103	Group of ecclesiastical enamels (KENNETH F. BATES)	156
A-R	Design ideas for enameling from simple to more complex motifs	157, 158, 159

EXPERIMENTS, SUGGESTIONS FOR NEW USES AND EARNING A LIVING BY ENAMELING

104	Pillbox (KENNETH F. BATES)	162
105	Silver box (KENNETH F. BATES)	163
106	*Big Top Celebrities* (KENNETH F. BATES)	165
107	*Marine Fantasy* (KENNETH F. BATES)	167
108	*Arabesque* (KENNETH F BATES)	170
109	Glass objects used in enameling	171
110	Silver goblet with *plique-à-jour* insets	172
111	Wall light with *plique-à-jour*	173
112	Enameled bracelet and ring	174
113	*Midsummer Night* (KENNETH F. BATES)	175
114	Stacking the kiln for mass firing	177
115	Group of enameled objects (KENNETH F. BATES)	178

CONTEMPORARY AMERICAN ENAMELISTS

A	*Side Show* (ARTHUR AMES)	180
B	Enamel plate (JEAN AMES)	181
C	Enamel jewelry (VIRGIL CANTINI)	182
D	Enamel plate (KARL DRERUP)	182
E	Enamel necklace (WILLIAM DEHART)	183
F	*Andante in Blue* (DORIS HALL)	184
G	*Altar Cross* (CHARLES BARTLEY JEFFERY)	185

LIST OF ILLUSTRATIONS

H	Enamel figure (MIZI OTTEN)	page	186
I	Enamel portrait (LISEL SALZER)		186
J	Enamel boxes and bowls (HAROLD TISHLER)		187
K	Enamel bracelet (MILDRED WATKINS)		187
L	*Angel Fish* (H EDWARD WINTER)		188
M	Enamel plaques (ELLAMARIE AND JACKSON WOOLLEY)		188

FOREWORD

THE SPREAD of America's artistic Renaissance during the past two generations is still an unexplained phenomenon. With all its complexities and apparent contradictions it is difficult to see, much less comprehend, in its proper perspective. But those of us who are historians and at the same time concerned with the education of artists cannot escape the issue. We must accept the responsibility of the past and the challenge of the future. It is our obligation to clarify the means by which the two are connected so that a continuous flow and organic growth of a genuine cultural expression is assured.

If we make the attempt to analyze the contemporary situation in American art, we would probably discover an amazing vitality taking form in two distinct phases. one through the progressive enterprise and experimentation of individual artists, and the other through the actual participation by the millions in some form of art as a popular expression.

Enameling is not yet a popular art in the literal sense, but it is rapidly becoming so, since modern industry has brought the price of the necessary equipment and materials within the reach of a larger public The aesthetic delight we get from its brilliant and iridescent color is one of the objectives of our most venturesome artists in the field of modern painting Its enjoyment is not limited to the few, but is the common endowment of all who take part in any form of visual pleasure Indeed, one of the handicaps to the more popular acceptance of the contemporary point of view, with its emphasis on spontaneity, strong design and brilliant color, has been its apparent preoccupation with painting, whereas in reality the artists who have extended this interest into the various hand and industrial crafts have made remarkable progress in almost every section of the country.

ENAMELING: *Principles and Practice*

A textbook on one of the oldest arts in the history of man, yet one of the least developed in terms of contemporary usage and style, seems to be a monumental achievement. Moreover, it is written by an artist who has himself made the transition from design as sheer personal expression to one which is intensified through a relatively unexplored medium and enriched by a wider social function. In bridging the gap between the professional and more specialized artist and the enormous numbers of technically gifted and artistically sensitive popular artists, we need more of this kind of leadership.

The world of this generation looks to America for leadership in matters of artistic expression as well as political and social well being. The cynicism of critics notwithstanding, we have accepted that leadership. For if we regard the visual arts in terms of both their intrinsic form and their function in society, and survey our achievements in architectural and industrial design as well as the so-called "fine arts" of painting, sculpture, ceramics, enameling and metalry, we have already set the pattern of the Twentieth Century.

An exhibition of enamels held at the University of Pittsburgh in March 1950 presented a magnificent array of famous pieces from the Seventh Century to the present. It was no accident that the outstanding examples of contemporary enamels were products of American artists, and most of these came from Cleveland.

Cleveland's prominence as an enameling center has a number of contributing factors in its immediate background. One is the presence in the Cleveland Museum of Art of a large portion of the Guelph Treasure, with its famous examples of medieval enamels and goldsmith work, which is the core around which a remarkable collection of late medieval and Renaissance enamels has been built. A second factor is the strong tradition of support by the Cleveland public to local artists through the purchase of their work not only in painting but also the crafts and particularly enamels Demoralization by machine production is a constant threat and it is largely by this tangible expression of interest that many an artist feels justified in making the necessary sacrifices to produce and develop articles of genuine quality. The third

Foreword

factor is the presence of Kenneth Bates and the group of artist-craftsmen who developed with him at the Cleveland Institute of Art over a period of nearly twenty-five years.

Born in North Scituate, near Boston, Massachusetts, in 1904, Bates came to Cleveland as instructor in design at the Institute of Art, then known as the Cleveland School of Art, in 1927. His artistic training had been at the Massachusetts School of Art, particularly under the American enamelist Laurin A. Martin, and the School of Fine Arts at Fontainebleau, France, with the inspiring Claude Lemuenier.

Bates's initial entry of an enameled bowl in the annual May Show at the Cleveland Museum of Art in 1928 won him first prize. From then on he has been a consistent winner of top honors in friendly competition with Edward Winter, Mildred Watkins, Doris Hall and others of the Cleveland enamelist group. Recognition outside his own environment has been almost equally generous; he received first prize in enameling in the Syracuse National Ceramic Exhibition in 1946, and has had his work exhibited in museums in several European countries and throughout the United States and purchased by many of them for their permanent collections.

It has frequently been said that ideas have consequences, and in the case of this artist they are of no small importance in this age of machine and mass production. Somewhere in his New England background he was indoctrinated with the idea that genuine artistic creation cannot be duplicated. The world of the machine and the commercial exploitation of an artist's inventions are therefore outside his range of interests. Sensitive perhaps to the point of preciousness, his work is small in size and designed to be seen as something unique and individual. Most objects are designed for the home or as jewelry for personal adornment, yet it seems logical that he should develop this interest in the ecclesiastical field where the work of art serves a more definite and devotional function.

As sources of inspiration this artist has frequently acknowledged his indebtedness to the fine examples of medieval enamels in American public collections. More important to him, however,

ENAMELING: *Principles and Practice*

have been the intricate craftsmanship and sensitive design of the Chinese tradition, particularly the gold and silver enamel work of the Ming dynasty. Perhaps more important than either of these is his own special hobby of horticulture, for many of the prize-winning flowers which he frequently exhibits in professional competitions are used as a basis for his designs in enamel.

Along with his art and his hobby Kenneth Bates has a long record of successful teaching at the Cleveland Institute of Art, and it is this experience with people of all types, skills and temperaments that helps make this book so important to both layman and the trained artist He holds back no trade secrets and gives his directions almost exactly as if you were working in the studio with him. The possibilities of the fine art of enameling are unlimited and this book will go a long way toward realizing them.

LAURENCE SCHMECKEBIER
Director, Cleveland Institute of Art

February 1951

INTRODUCTION

ENAMELING on metal is not difficult. It is an exacting art which demands careful attention to such details as cleaning, application and firing, but it cannot be called "hard to do." In my opinion a technical process such as enameling becomes as "easy" or "hard" to do as the one doing it makes it for himself. If one proposes to be an artist, he never considers such an ambiguous term, but works with only one idea in mind; that is, to finish to his own satisfaction the present piece of work so that he may be released to start the next. There can be no termination to art endeavor, for, especially after finishing an enamel, there are always variations of color, texture and motif which come to one's mind. The process of making and firing an enamel, therefore, constitutes a truly creative activity.

Enameling on metal is variable but not entirely unpredictable. The manufacturer of enameled merchandise or the commercial producer must discover color recipes and temperatures for firing which will enable him to turn out scores of identical kitchen ranges or other utilitarian objects, whereas the artist-craftsman has no such concern. He is not desirous of developing his art into an exacting science. On the contrary, the student in his laboratory or the artist in his studio takes great delight in variations and subtle nuances of glistening hues, as his enamels come from the kiln never quite the same.

In this age of rapid movement, both in production and consumption, people need relief from nervous tensions. It is no new argument that the controlled and sustained effort of some handcraft achieves this end, yet there is always the misconception that it is slow and tedious work to produce a handmade object. The craftsman absorbed in his work finds that it is no compromise to place quality ahead of speed. Rapidly done and care-

ENAMELING. *Principles and Practice*

lessly thought-out enamels are quite useless. They merely reflect an attempt to beat the machine at its own game Why not sit down and make, from beginning to end, a beautiful creation which will give one pride in his own accomplishment and which will be cherished by someone else? This creation is bound to involve time It cannot be hurried It will take time to invent the design motif, to relate the color juxtapositions and choices, to fire properly and to bring to a successful finish the object which heretofore existed only in the imagination.

"How to do it" can be taught in a few "easy" lessons. That part I will explain in this book, but what you do with the knowledge will differ from what your fellow artist will do with the same knowledge. This is the unpredictable ingredient of art called "creativeness."

In setting down the established principles of enameling and offering a few suggestions for individual experimentation in this field, I am in no way trying to compete with the many books which cover so completely the historical background of the subject. Furthermore, it is my wish to introduce only enough of the technical side of chemistry, glaze composition and mechanical engineering to be of practical use to the artist.

My work as instructor of design and enameling leads me to believe that the thrill which comes to a student as he finishes his first piece is of paramount importance and should be recognized. His development as an artist depends largely upon his ability to experience over and over again these original excitements. Later explorations into more technical refinements are, in my opinion, of less importance. It is because of my intention to allow the beginner to capture such an initial thrill and then progress to more ambitious endeavors that I have purposely kept the discussion of making a simple tray free from complicated and involved styles in enameling

My own first inspirations in the field of enameling were experienced while in the classes of Laurin A. Martin at the Massachusetts School of Art in 1924. Here, as a student, I felt a kind of awesome enchantment when the master unwrapped glowing and colorful creations which had been painstakingly conceived

Introduction

in his own studio. These pieces created an acquisitive feeling in the observer. At this time I was convinced that a good piece of craftsmanship is readily spotted by many who desire to possess it. The owner not only wants to see it more often, but he wants to hold and handle it. Much can be said, therefore, about quality, finish and tactile values which I will leave to later chapters of this book.

After my studies at the Massachusetts School of Art, I came to the Cleveland Institute of Art in 1927 to teach design. In the following year, I traveled through many countries in Europe and found lasting inspiration from the rare and exquisite examples of medieval enamels at the Cluny Museum and at the Louvre. A most impressive exhibition of Byzantine cloisonné work at the Musée des Arts Décoratif in Paris thoroughly assured me that here was a medium which held every challenge and enticement for one interested in color, craftsmanship and design. Soon after my return from abroad I decided to take up the study and production of enameling as a life work.

I have tried different methods of introducing this work to students but the experiment used with a class of painters was of singular interest. We started to make enamels with only brief preliminary discussion of techniques, firing tests and history. The students used the medium in much the same way they had used their paints, with no inhibitions or fear of mistakes. The results were surprisingly good and showed much more freedom in design expression than more carefully planned problems, along with some unusual, and even unorthodox, enamel effects. I have used the same kind of direct approach to the art of enameling in this book.

I wish to acknowledge my indebtedness to Laurence Schmeckebier, who has been a guiding spirit and helpful adviser in the construction of this book; to my good friends, John Paul Miller and Richard Godfrey, for their skill and unerring taste in photographing the enameling processes; to the Cleveland Institute of Art and the many students there who are a constant incentive; to the Cleveland Museum of Art and its director, Mr. William M. Milliken, for the cooperation and generosity shown; to the

INTRODUCTION

Metropolitan Museum of Art, the Taft Museum in Cincinnati, the Cleveland Public Library; to all of my distinguished contemporaries who so kindly submitted photographs of their work; to Jean McKechnie, whose brilliant editing warrants unending praise, and to my wife Charlotte, who is my art critic and my inspiration.

KENNETH F. BATES

I

A BRIEF HISTORY OF ENAMELING: Greek enamels · Celtic enamels · Byzantine enamels· German enamels · French enamels · Enameled portraits · English enamels · Russian enamels · Chinese and Japanese enamels · English revival in 1864 · Viennese school · Enameling in America

THERE IS probably no art technique in common use in this country today that has to be more constantly explained to the public than the technique of enameling on metal In European countries the art of enameling and its heritage are recognized. However, in America the word "enamel" is also used to mean resinous paint for decorating kitchen chairs, brightly colored lacquer for a lady's fingernails, a superior automobile finish or the outer covering of our teeth. To the artist, enameling means only one thing—the process of applying a thin coat of glass to a metal which, when heated to high temperatures, melts and becomes fused to the metal.

GREEK ENAMELS

Enameling has been known since the Fifth Century B.C. Pieces of Greek sculpture of that period show areas of inlaid gold covered with a form of glaze which was enamel One example of this is the gold drapery on the Phidias statue of Zeus which was enameled with figures and flowers.

In the Fourth Century B.C. we find proof that the ancient Greek goldsmiths inlaid flowers and other small designs with a thin coating of white or pale blue enamel between slightly raised outlines of gold wire. This process, known as *cloisonné*, must be accepted as the forerunner to all other enameling processes.

ENAMELING: *Principles and Practice*

Some historians insist that on Egyptian jewelry, ornaments and small images of mummies areas of inlaid enamel can be found, but it would seem more accurate to describe them as areas filled with crushed, colored stones which were held in place by some adhesive. Not having been subjected to heat and, therefore, not actually fused to the metal, we cannot rightfully call these examples of enamels, although the appearance of texture, color and technique is certainly misleading. Glassmaking was practiced by the Egyptians as early as 1300 B.C. Glazes on tiles and pottery have also been found but no examples of glaze applied to metals.

Fig 1 Christ, German Medallion from Franken, Eighth Century, A.D (*Courtesy Cleveland Museum of Art*)

CELTIC ENAMELS

To the Celts of the British Isles of the Third Century A.D. is attributed some of our earliest records of enamel work. These warriors were known to have poured molten colors into bronze molds which hardened and formed filigrees for decorating their shields and swords. This method of pouring enamel into sunken or gouged areas in the metal is known as champlevé enamel. The Celts and Saxons of a later period from the Sixth to the Ninth Century A.D. left numerous examples of this type of poured

A Brief History of Enameling

molten glass. The colors, those which have not suffered by deterioration, show that they used mainly lapis blue, strong red and white.

In the British Museum are both Roman and Celtic pieces of champlevé work on bronze. Other collections are found in the Cluny Museum, the Louvre, the Victoria and Albert Museum and many American museums. In the enamels of this early Christian era the art student as well as the historian will find much of interest (*Fig.* 1)

BYZANTINE ENAMELS

Under just what circumstances the making of enamel work was transferred from the northern countries to Byzantium is not known, but the art flourished there from the latter part of the Ninth Century until the Eleventh Century (*Fig.* 2). The Byzantine enamels were of the cloisonné type, differing from

Fig. 2 Byzantine enamel, Eighth Century, A.D. This is possibly the rarest enamel in the whole Byzantine collection. It is the cover of a reliquary of the True Cross supposedly brought back by a Crusader from the Near East. (*Courtesy Metropolitan Museum of Art*)

ENAMELING: *Principles and Practice*

the champlevé types of the earlier Merovingian and barbaric enamels The objects were mainly done on fine beaten gold and the thin wires, or cloisons, which separated one color from another, were often not more than 1/100 inch thick It is amazing how well these examples have been preserved Had it not been for the fact that so much work in this period was made of gold, more extensive collections would exist today Since gold was valuable, invaders from all parts of the world carried off many enamels to be melted and reused. When he views the extant examples, a present-day craftsman can hardly forget that he is creating in a medium which will retain its original quality for over one thousand years. One outstanding example, the famous Pala d'Oro, can be seen in St Mark's Cathedral, Venice, where it was transported from Constantinople in 1105.

The peak of Byzantine enameling was reached in the Tenth and Eleventh Centuries. Before this time much of the work was small or used only as accents set between more heavily jeweled objects, such as in bracelets, crowns, brooches and finger rings. The very earliest Byzantine enamels were merely tiny jewel-like pieces or beads made to be set or sewn wherever desired.

The beautiful cloisonné work of the Byzantines also suggests a Persian derivation A possible theory is that the art of enameling spread westward to Byzantium from Persia, the northern Caucasus, Egypt, Asia Minor, South Russia and the Danube and, at the same time, eastward from the British Isles.

To select for discussion only a few pieces from the wealth of enamels which are genuinely Byzantine, or have a Byzantine character (*Fig* 3), is not an easy task. However, there is not room enough to list all of them. Superb examples remain in the Church of St Sophia at Constantinople and at St Mark's in Venice Among the most famous collections of Byzantine enamels is the J. Pierpont Morgan collection in the Metropolitan Museum of New York City. The beautiful colored photographs of this group are almost as stimulating as the objects themselves. At first glance, the Byzantine work appears stiff and formal, until one realizes a powerful inner composition dominating the formal posture and expression of the personalities portrayed. This for-

A Brief History of Enameling

Fig. 3 Two champlevé plaques, French Limoges, first half of the Twelfth Century The character of the animals as well as the bold contrasting colors reflect the Byzantine character (*Courtesy Metropolitan Museum of Art*)

mality was dictated by the church and could not be cast aside by the artisan. Probably no other period in the history and development of the Christian religion influenced the artist so strongly. Close examination of these enamels discloses that they are almost hieroglyphic in character and represent a distinct type of design.

The spread of the art of enameling now becomes more definite. Historians all agree that it was Theophano, a Byzantine princess, who introduced the art in Germany when she married their king Otto II. She had such a love for the beautiful enamel work of her family and her native land that she decided to bring enamel craftsmen with her to Europe There she established artisans who worked in gold using the same type of design they had used in Byzantium.

GERMAN ENAMELS

The character of all the early work in the Western world was strongly Byzantine. Artists in one town in Germany would spread the knowledge and traditions of the craft to the next. Thus we find the same methods and designs used in monastery after monastery all along the valleys of the Rhine and the Meuse, through the towns of Saxony, Brunswick and others (*Fig.* 4)

ENAMELING: *Principles and Practice*

Of all the remaining examples of this important period in Germany before enameling spread to France, none is more impressive and more valuable to historian and artist alike than the great treasure started by the family of Guelph. The Cleveland Museum

Fig. 4 The Baptism and the Crucifixion, Mosan school, Twelfth Century. Enameling of this period often showed the use of the cloisonné and the champlevé techniques combined (*Courtesy Metropolitan Museum of Art*)

A Brief History of Enameling

of Art is renowned for its possession of many articles which once belonged to this famous treasure (*Fig* 5). The whole story of the treasure is a fascinating tale It started when Countess Gertrudis I presented a cross in memory of her husband to the Cathedral of St Blasius After her death in 1077, the portable altars, crosses, reliquaries, monstrances, caskets and other exquisite examples of the enameler's art were added to the collection.

Fig. 5 The first and second Gertrudis crosses and the Gertrudis Portable Altar, three pieces from the fabulous Guelph Treasure. German, Brunswick, Lower Saxony, about 1040. (*Courtesy Cleveland Museum of Art*)

Later Duke Henry the Lion brought back relics from the Second Crusade to add to the treasure. He also had goldsmiths make other pieces similar to those seen on his travels and these, too, were included in the collection. In 1218, Otto IV bequeathed to the Cathedral all examples of enameling done before 1200 that he considered to be important. As late as 1528, at the time of the Reformation, the relics were being carefully preserved. Additions

ENAMELING *Principles and Practice*

of possibly less merit artistically continued to be made until the middle of the Sixteenth Century

Signatures of famous goldsmiths preserved on their works increase the value of this treasure The Eilbertus altar ascertains that he is without doubt one of the greatest goldsmiths and enamelers of the Twelfth Century This altar is also one of the best preserved pieces of all medieval enamels.

Cloisonné was common knowledge as was champlevé and gilding (*Fig* 6) Sometimes the craftsman was not satisfied to use

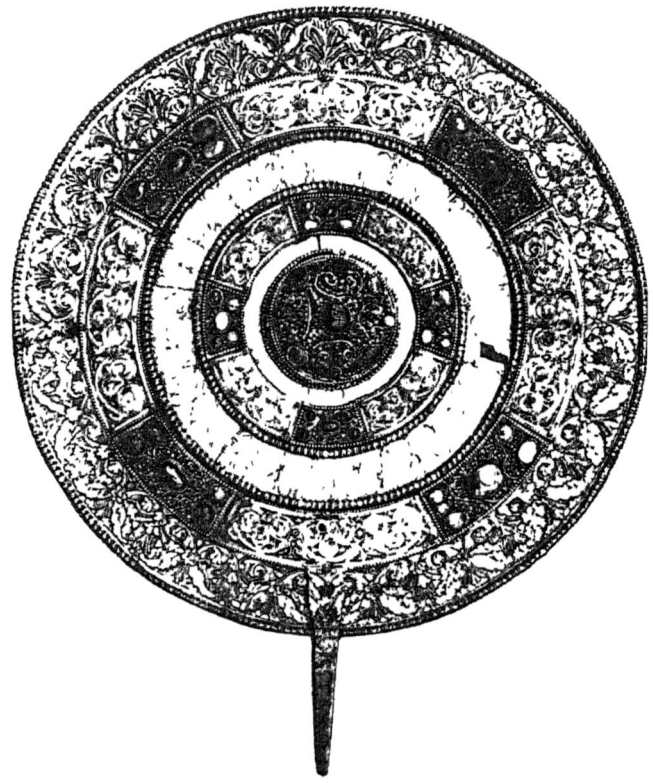

Fig 6 A flabellum, or fan, Rhenish, 1200. These fans were twelve inches in diameter and were held by two deacons standing on either side of the altar They were often richly decorated with champlevé enamel as they were in this case. (*Courtesy Metropolitan Museum of Art*)

A Brief History of Enameling

only one technique, but used the champlevé to inlay a bold pattern in the background and worked the fine lines of the cloisonné method into his figures and animals. This kind of mixed work is later in date than the pure champlevé and shows a logical transition from the simple to the more complicated. The use of bronze effected a new development in enameling. It necessitated the use of opaque colors instead of the transparent ones because the constituent of tin alloys in bronze made the colors too cloudy. Today enameling on bronze is rarely done by the handcraftsman.

FRENCH ENAMELS

Not until shortly before 1500 did the next change in enameling take place Because this new type of work developed and flourished in the French town of Limoges, the method is often referred to as Limoges enamel. A more complete discussion of Limoges enamel will be covered in a later chapter, so we will describe it here only as the process of painting with enamel on the surface of metal Of course, there were several phases of development before the craftsmen arrived at the method now used.

It was customary in medieval times for a family to work at one certain craft. One family worked in competition with another, and family pride and honor were more important than individual skill. In the case of enameling, it was the family of Penicaud, according to most historians, which won over its competitors. Léonard Penicaud, sometimes called "Nardon," was first in line His innovation was first to cover the entire plate of copper with an opaque white enamel and then proceed to draw on it with a black oxide. After this step had been fired he applied his transparent enamels, using several layers and eventually using opaque white again in different gradations to give the effect of a modeled surface. Lastly, thin layers of violet enamel were fired and all sorts of delightful details developed.

The work of Nardon's brother Jean, known to historians as Penicaud II, was the first to show the use of transparent colors on copper. His work consisted mainly of ecclesiastical enamels in the form of diptychs, triptychs and polyptychs.

ENAMELING: *Principles and Practice*

ENAMELED PORTRAITS

The names of Léonard Limousin *(Fig. 7)* and Pierre Reymond *(Fig. 8)* stand out as the great enamelists of the Sixteenth Century. Both of these artists carried the work in enameling still

Fig. 7 Portrait of François de Cleves, LEONARD LIMOUSIN, Sixteenth Century. One of the important personages at the Court of Henry II of France. *(Courtesy The Taft Museum, Cincinnati)*

A Brief History of Enameling

Fig 8 *The Month of May*, PIERRE REYMOND, French Limoges, 1513 (*Courtesy The Taft Museum, Cincinnati*)

further. Equipped with greater skill and complete control of the medium, they developed the art of portraiture in enamels.

Portraiture is a type of enameling not often executed today. Enamel portraits are achieved by the use of delicately ground enamel tints and require many careful firings for building up flesh tones and anatomical likenesses. A comprehensive collection, and, indeed, one of the most important collections, of this kind of work can be seen at the Taft Museum in Cincinnati, Ohio.

These famous Sixteenth-Century artisans made the back of a piece as beautiful if not more intriguing than the front. I am convinced that more objects of rare antiquity and great value should be handled, at least by those who appreciate them. Their tactile quality is a vital part of their message I realize this is a very impractical thought and we might not have all of these valuable collections if everyone were to handle the museum treasures.

ENAMELING: *Principles and Practice*

However, in teaching the subject of enamel and metal craft one of the primary requirements is that it must not be unpleasant to touch, regardless of its visual appeal This fact must have been known by the early craftsmen for there is rarely an example of enameling done by them which does not verify the principle of the importance of tactility

Of course, not all of the pieces done at this time meet with even the most lenient standards of good design and color. Some are very bad and show nothing of the ability in drawing and composition of the masters.

The spread of the art of enamel portraiture was rapid, but the quality of work eventually showed a decline. We find enamelers tended more and more toward making copies of paintings. The great portraits of the Limousin era gave way to pretty miniatures on fancy snuff boxes and mirrors during the reigns of Francis I and Louis XIV (*Fig.* 9)

Fig. 9 *Mirror—Juno,* painted enamel, French Limoges, late Sixteenth Century.

A Brief History of Enameling

ENGLISH ENAMELS

In England the factories at Battersea, developed by Stephan Theodore Jansen in 1750 and flourishing until 1820, produced quantities of small boxes (*Figs* 10 and 11) and dishes mostly decorated with pink and white enamels which depicted Watteau-esque gentlemen and ladies surrounded by misty woodland scenes. Designs and motifs were eventually printed instead of hand drawn and very little which could be called art resulted.

Fig. 10 Small enameled *étui,* or needlecase, English, Staffordshire, Eighteenth Century. *(Courtesy Metropolitan Museum of Art)*

Fig. 11 Enameled *nécessaire,* or workbox, English, Bilston (?), Eighteenth Century. *(Courtesy Metropolitan Museum of Art)*

RUSSIAN ENAMELS

Not much mention is made by historians of the important and quite different type of enameling done by the Russians. This is

ENAMELING · *Principles and Practice*

a type of wire enamel known as *plique-à-jour* or backless enamel. characterized by predominantly transparent colors It may well have developed from the Byzantine. By adding elaborate twisted, braided or filigreed wire the Russians and South Slavonic peoples attained a different, rather dazzling effect Although the *plique-à-jour* technique was tried by the Renaissance workers in France and Italy, the most interesting examples of this type were done by the Russians Necklaces, chains and demitasse spoons are cherished examples of this work When held to the light they give a rich jewel-like appearance, suggesting tiny stained-glass windows

CHINESE AND JAPANESE ENAMELS

We have no authentic record that enamels were done to any extent in China before the Thirteenth Century This event coincides with the Mongolian invasion and it is said that a number of artificers set up shop as they traveled across Asia, just as invaders from Syria brought the arts of Byzantium to France The Chinese enamels, almost exclusively cloisonné, were copied and profusely carried out by the Japanese from 1596 onward (*Fig* 12).

What household at the turn of the century—and most attics still have several examples—couldn't produce at least one or two Oriental cloisonné vases, boxes or trays? Everyone is familiar with the odd-shaped, long-necked urns with typical Japanese motifs, such as a graceful crane among reeds or some white chrysanthemums and green leaves on a black background and the inevitable Japanese fret or the cloud motif. Only after seeing examples of the finer pieces of this work in museums is it possible to detect any differences. The numerous tiny wires, each one as thin as a hair, had to be placed there by hand and, to this day, it seems incredible that these well-executed cloisonné enamels can be sold for a dollar or two.

Another point in regard to the enamels is that in the inferior piece there can be detected tiny pits caused by the use of much softer enamels and less careful attention to the ends of scrolls in the cloisonné work Often the Japanese give a final finish by

A Brief History of Enameling

Fig 12 An example of the exquisite early Japanese cloisonné enameling made in the Sixteenth and Seventeenth Centuries.

ENAMELING: *Principles and Practice*

rubbing with fine files and eliminate the firing after the stoning process. This gives an eggshell finish rather than the more commonly seen high glossy surface

ENGLISH REVIVAL IN 1864

From 1864 until about 1910 there was a revival of the enameling art in England. I mention but three names in the list of a dozen or more who contributed to this revival They are Alexander Fisher, Harold Stabler and H. H Cunynghame. Alexander Fisher is best known both for his rather realistic portraits and his allegorical subjects The high quality of his work approached that of the early Renaissance master, Penicaud Judged by our present standards of taste, the work shows greater skill with the medium than in proficiency of design. He excelled in combining precious metals and jewels with the Limoges type of painted enamels Many examples of his work still exist in this country

Harold Stabler, another English enameler, used a purely decorative style, although his work also reflected a design typical of the 1900 period—stiff, highly conventional and sentimental in character. The work of both Stabler and Fisher fitted in perfectly with the Pre-Raphaelite school of art

H H Cunynghame's book *Art of Enamelling on Metals*, written in 1899, must have added greatly to the interest in enameling current at the time. Even today his book is as complete and thorough a treatise on the subject as can be found. He speaks of enamels "easy to make by the whitest of fingers in the most tidy of drawing rooms." It was a time of battle for those valiant Pre-Raphaelite thinkers who were terrified at the oncoming march of the monster called the "machine." Cunynghame and others of the period tried desperately to hold on to a few of the traditions of the handmade object. Enameling as a handcraft was being jeopardized, and one admires their fight to preserve it. They lost their battle with the manufacturer and the machine for many decades to come, but the periodical revivals in this craft prove that their mission was not entirely in vain. The unique handmade piece of craftwork as well as the factory-made commercial piece finds a market today. It is merely sold on a different counter.

A Brief History of Enameling

VIENNESE SCHOOL

In 1929 the Vienna School of Arts and Crafts held its sixtieth anniversary in the Austrian Museum of Art and Industry This exhibition marked, along with other progressive movements in all the fields of crafts, a decided revival of the work in enameling on metal. To quote from *Austrian Applied Arts,* by L. W. Rochowanski (Heinz and Company, Vienna, c1930), an illustrated book which has been a source of great inspiration to many art students in the last decade, "The Vienna School of Arts and Crafts has become world famous The list of painters, sculptors, architects and other craftsmen who have graduated from it contains many names of note, while its students come from every quarter of the globe It is the center, the nursery of applied art!"

Through the influence of the Vienna School of Arts and Crafts enameling took on a different aspect Metal figures and enameled twisted copper animals were given a coat of gay opaque colors, fired and enhanced in their charm by addition of simple geometric spots of silver and gold foil Directly attributed to this school in Vienna are the trays, boxes and brooches which are characterized by plain, smooth areas of enamel Up to this time it would be hard to find enamels of this kind The French, German, Oriental and English examples were predominantly pictorial New ideas in home decoration, architecture and fashion in general created a desire for the machinelike precision and severity of hard-edged geometric style. The Vienna School showed that machine methods could be utilized by the American artist without sacrificing aesthetic qualities The present wave of popularity (1929-1950) is akin to the Arts and Crafts Movement of the 1900 period. From the small ash'tray to the ambitious collector's items, the medium of enamel has been accepted by craftsmen as a legitimate and challenging vehicle of expression.

ENAMELING IN AMERICA

The National Ceramic Exhibition of enamels as well as pottery was founded in 1932 in memory of Adelaide Alsop Robineau and held in Syracuse, New York. It is sponsored by the Syracuse

ENAMELING: *Principles and Practice*

Museum of Fine Arts and the Onondaga Potteries, and circulated annually throughout the country In 1937 it was officially invited to Denmark, Sweden, Finland and England, being the first American Ceramic exhibition ever to be invited abroad. The Golden Gate International Exposition held in San Francisco in 1939 also invited the Exhibition to appear there To such museums as the Syracuse Museum and the Cleveland Museum of Art. with its annual May Show, goes much credit for bringing the enameler's creations out of his studio and placing them in the hands of the consumer At the same time, these annual exhibitions have established an incentive for the craftsman to put forth his best efforts.

II

HOW ENAMELS ARE COMPOUNDED AND ENAMELING TOOLS AND MATERIALS: Types of enamels · Silica · Oxide of lead · Borax · Potash and soda · Oxides of metal · Materials · Kilns · Tools · Gum tragacanth

BEFORE ACTUALLY beginning the first piece of enamel work, I would like to discuss first the types of enamel which can be used and the component parts which go to make up various enamels. The elaborate process of compounding enamel is not practical for the average craftsman today, for the time needed to do this would make the finished enamel prohibitive in price The finest old enamels found in many museums were not only designed and fired by the famous craftsmen but each separate color was manufactured by them Here the modern artist has the advantage of being able to utilize the products of manufacturers. Just as the painter need not be delayed in his work by having to make his paints, so the enamelist can use ready-made materials. A complete treatise on the manufacture of enamel can be found in more technical books* for those who wish to experiment in this field

TYPES OF ENAMELS

There are four types of enamel made commercially: the opaques, the transparents or translucents, the opalescents and the overglazes or overpainting enamels. Opaque enamels are solid colors that do not permit light to pass through, whereas light does pass through the transparents and translucents. In the latter category is included what is called "flux," a clear, colorless enamel which is the basis for all colored enamels.

---

* *Art Enamelling on Metals*, by H. H Cunynghame, Westminster, 1899, is one of the most complete treatises.

ENAMELING. *Principles and Practice*

Opalescent enamels are transparents having a clouded or milky appearance These are rarer than the other enamels. In many of the fine old French pieces done in the Fifteenth and Sixteenth Centuries and, more often, in the later English pieces of the Eighteenth Century, one may find small areas of enamel which are neither transparent nor opaque. The effect is iridescent like that of an opal.

Old-fashioned china-painting colors, or overglaze, are used in some instances for detail work, applied with either pen or brush over a previously fired enamel surface

For general work in enameling and until the craftsman has acquired sufficient skill, the first two types are quite adequate With an unlimited number of opaques and a wide range of transparents plus the opportunity for varying these colors as they are applied over different metals, the enamelist is already inspired with a tempting and colorful palette All types of enamel may be purchased either in an unground state. called frit, or ground to any desired degree of fineness. This fineness is designated in terms of the mesh through which the particles of enamel will pass. Overglazes are actually enamels ground to a fine dust In order to make use of the overglaze colors, they must first be suspended in some volatile oil such as oil of sassafras, oil of lavender or a drop of pure turpentine. To extend the colors a tiny amount of squeegee oil is added. These two vehicles and the powdered enamel are then carefully mixed on a glass or agate slab with a flexible palette knife until a perfectly smooth paste has been attained.

Unfortunately, new shades and hues cannot be produced by the mere process of mixing two enamels. If this were the case, only a small number of enamels would be required and every known variation could be produced by the admixture of these. However, each color is composed of a different proportion of fluxes and oxides and is produced under different conditions. Occasionally, I have had to resort to grinding several colors together in a mortar with the pestle in order to procure an exact value or tone. What invariably happens then is that when fired, the tiny particles of each color will show as specks rather than a homogeneous new color.

How Enamels Are Compounded — Tools and Materials

SILICA

As we explained at the beginning of this book, enamel is really colored glass composed of silicates. Glass, porcelain, earthenware, bricks, tiles and crockery are all silicates of varying composition. Silica, or sand, is colorless when pure. It has many peculiar qualities, one being that when heated with soda, magnesia, potash and lime, or with oxides of lead or iron, it becomes a fused mass of glass or slag. Potash or soda plus lime in conjunction with silica in the proper proportions produces clear glass. The presence of iron or lead oxide colors the glass slightly.

OXIDE OF LEAD

Softness and hardness of enamel is determined by the amount of oxide of lead present. A high content of oxide of lead produces a soft enamel. This is important since the enamel must have a lower melting point than the metal to which it is applied. Its only disadvantage lies in the fact that soft enamels can become scratched very easily.

BORAX

Borax, too, creates a softer enamel, but it has an additional advantage since it enables the enamel to unite more easily with the oxides of different metals, which give enamels their color. The presence of too much borax in the enamel reduces its elasticity, the most convenient of all characteristics of enamel.

POTASH AND SODA

Potash and soda, both alkalis, are used in the manufacture of enamels. The bright, polished, sparkling effect of enamels is partly due to potash in their composition, while the presence of soda renders the enamel more elastic.

OXIDES OF METAL

So far I have discussed only the materials necessary for the

ENAMELING. *Principles and Practice*

making of clear, colorless enamel called flux. Used alone over copper, flux results in a warm shade of tan All of the colors, and there is no end to the number, are obtained by adding certain oxides of metals to this basic flux. Many of the rich colors used by the early Limoges masters, and even those used by the Byzantine artists, were essentially the same as those used today The deep transparent cobalt blue is made by mixing black oxide of cobalt with powdered flint glass. Other blues are obtained by using smaller proportions of oxide of cobalt It is the one color which people remember as an "enamel" color more than any other Blue enamels are satisfactory over pure copper, but highly flattered in their intensity when applied to pure silver. Oxide of copper produces the turquoise shades as well as some of the grass greens. Red enamels, either opaque or transparent, are obtained from gold oxide

Other colors are produced by using the following oxides platinum for soft grays, uranium and antimony for yellows, manganese for purples, oxides of tin for white, and iridium for a rich black. Opalescent enamels are compounded much the same as transparents, with the addition of more oxide of tin to increase the opacity.

Having combined the proper silicates with given amounts of oxides for coloring, the materials are placed into a melting furnace. After fifteen hours of steady heat, a process known as fritting, the art enamel is usually poured onto cold iron slabs in pancakelike forms.

If the craftsman prefers to grind the colors by hand, he may buy the frit in the unground, or chunk, state Commercially ground enamels are pulverized in large ball mills and then sifted or strained through sieves of various meshes. A convenient mesh for spatula work is 80 mesh. This means that the threads or wires through which the ground enamel is passed cross at the rate of 80 per square inch Sixty or 80 mesh enamel is about as coarse as table sugar or salt, while 200 mesh is more like flour.

In summary, enamel is made of the following: 1. silica (as sand), 2. borates (as borax, or borate of sodium), 3 alkalis

How Enamels Are Compounded — Tools and Materials

(as soda and potash), 4 alkaline earths (as lime, magnesia, lead) and 5 oxides of metals for coloring.

MATERIALS

Now that the various types of enamels and how they are compounded have been explained, the next step is to study the enameler's tools and their uses. Listed below are the basic materials needed by a beginner in enameling, which are illustrated in *Fig.* 13

> Two ounces each of fifteen different enamels ground to 80 mesh These should include: opaque black, opaque white, flux and the primary hues in both transparent and opaque enamels
>
> Fifteen two-ounce, screw-top ointment jars.
>
> A selection of small copper trays, either spun, stamped or hammered
>
> Spatula, pointer and spreader for applying enamel
>
> An ordinary nose-and-throat atomizer with an adjustable nozzle.
>
> Gum tragacanth solution.
>
> Fine steel wool, No. 00.
>
> Pyrex dishes for acid solutions.
>
> Ceramic stilts or stainless steel stands for firing.
>
> Two small glasses and syringe for washing enamels.
>
> Emery cloth for removing fire glaze.
>
> A one-third horsepower motor with spindles for buffing, and felt buffers, cotton buffers, tripoli and jeweler's rouge
>
> Long tongs or kitchen spatula.
>
> Large metal file and three small jeweler's files including rattail, round and half-round files.

ENAMELING: *Principles and Practice*

A variety of small bottles for dusting.

Fine mesh wire, No 100

Sable brushes, Nos. 8, 3 and 00.

Enameling kiln.

Asbestos mittens or gloves (needed only if large kiln is used).

A soft cotton rag.

Supplementary tools

Dogwood or rawhide mallet.

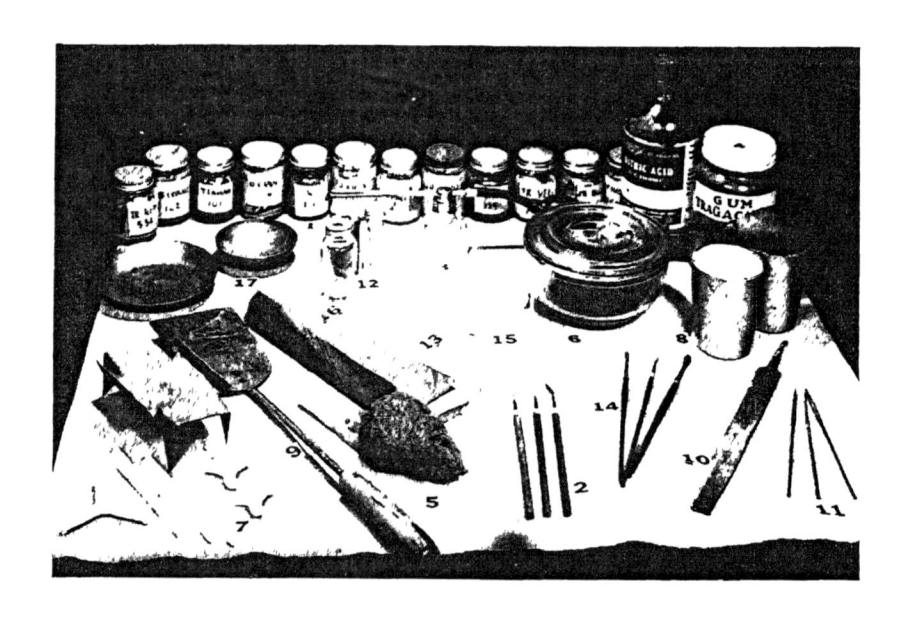

Fig. 13 Materials for the Beginner in Enameling   1. Enamels   2 Enamel tools   3. Atomizer   4. Gum tragacanth   5. Steel wool   6. Pyrex dish for acid solution   7 Stilts and stand   8. Glasses and syringe   9. Spatula   10 Large file   11. Small files   12. Dusting bottles   13 Wire mesh   14 Brushes   15. Rag   16. Emery cloth   17. Copper trays. NOTE. The kiln and buffing motor are not included.

How Enamels Are Compounded — Tools and Materials

Stake tree.

Planishing hammer.

Mushroom anvil or T stake.

Metal shears.

Dividers.

Blowtorch.

Charcoal or asbestos block.

Mortar and pestle.

The functions of most of the equipment in the above list will be explained along with the process of making a simple tray. A discussion of some of the required tools at this time may, however, be helpful.

KILNS

A kiln is nothing more than a small furnace which can be heated to extremely high temperatures. Many types of kiln are available on the market, ranging in price from $45.00 to $150.00 according to size and quality. Almost any type of kiln is satisfactory for firing enamels so long as it will reach a temperature of about 1500° F. in a reasonable length of time. Its size depends entirely on the individual needs of the craftsman and what he can afford to purchase. I have used kilns with an inside oven capacity varying from 3" high × 4" wide × 6" deep to an oven capacity of 28" × 36" × 40". The quality of the glazes achieved depends mainly on whether or not the heat is evenly distributed. Many small pieces can be made with the small kilns used by most laboratories for heat-treating (*Fig.* 14)

A kiln is not difficult to make yourself with, perhaps, some help from an electrician to install it. With any good, high-fired kiln brick, build up the proportions which will best suit your demands. A brick such as LW-10 or Corundite (trade names for refractory bricks) is excellent since it is sold in the convenient

ENAMELING: *Principles and Practice*

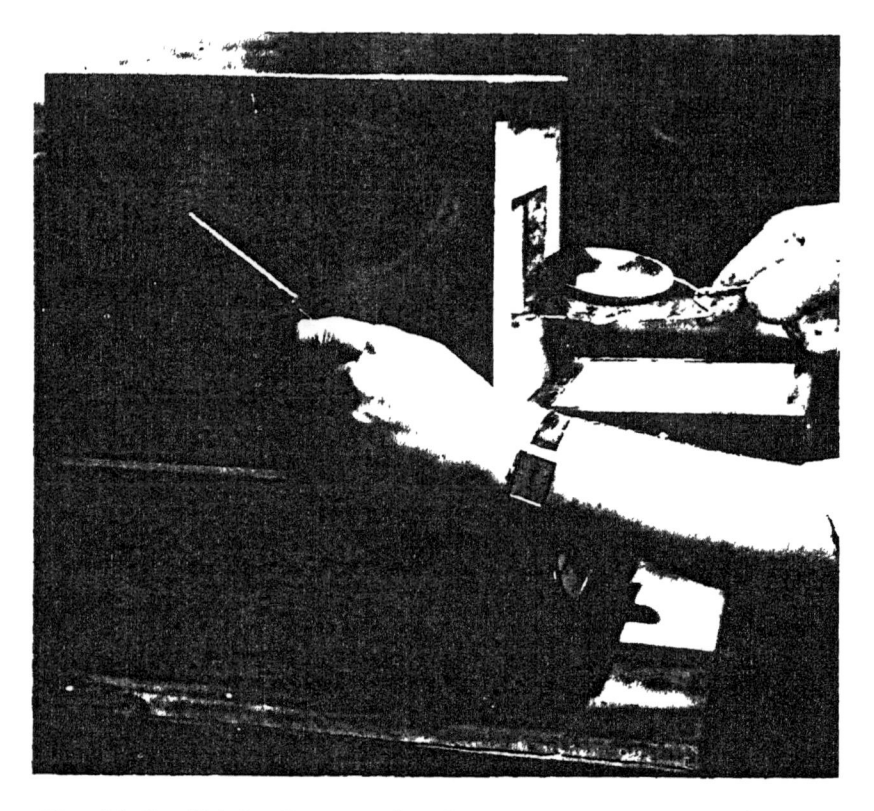

Fig. 14 Small kiln. Interior chamber measures 4 inches wide by 6 inches deep by 3½ inches high.

2" × 4" × 9" size. Lay the bricks as illustrated (*Fig.* 15) and leave the size opening you think you will need. Notice that all the walls and the top are 4" thick. This assures ample insulation although a castable refractory cement may be used between bricks for added insulation of your kiln. For the top you must have a slab of the same material large enough to bridge across the side walls. The door in the front can either be the type which works with a weight and pulley, or the plug-type door like the one pictured (*Fig.* 15). Whichever type of door is used, choose one which opens quickly and easily, for the process of enamel firing requires frequent observation. When the bricks are in place, coils meas-

How Enamels Are Compounded — Tools and Materials

uring half an inch in diameter of medium weight Nicrome wire are recessed in grooves around the floor of the kiln and around its ceiling. These are connected to a three-way switch (high, low, medium) on the outside of the kiln and you are ready to operate.

TOOLS

To apply enamel only three simple tools are necessary (*Fig. 16*), and these are not difficult to improvise from scraps of metal, wire and some hard wood dowels from the hardware store. A *pointer*, or jeweler's scribe, consists of a sharp-pointed piece of metal set into a wooden handle It is used both for tracing lines on the copper and for moving small particles of enamel into place. A *spatula* is a small tool with a flattened end similar to a tiny golf club This is used to lift the enamel from the container and place it on the copper A *spreader* is made by bending a

Fig 15 A homemade kiln (shown open with door on top). Interior chamber measures 12 inches wide by 12 inches deep by 5 inches high.

blunt, polished wire to an angle of about 135° from the handle, so that it lies on a horizontal surface when the handle is held as a pencil. It is used to maneuver the enamel into the design and also to spread it out and level it off. Dentist's tools, nut picks and jeweler's tools could be used as supplementary equipment, but the three tools described will be suitable for most purposes.

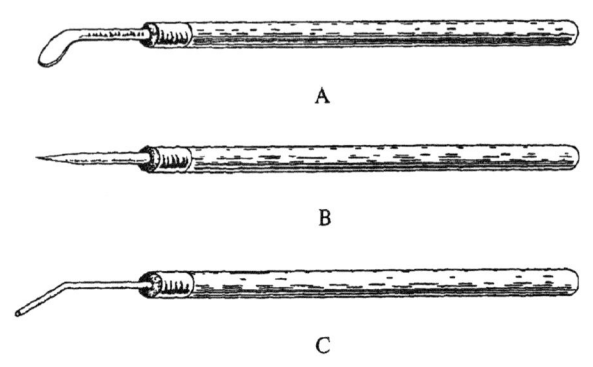

Fig 16 The Three Tools for Enameling   A The SPATULA is used for picking up moist enamel from the jar   B. The POINTER is used for placing the enamel and also for scratching lines   C. The SPREADER is used for leveling the enamel.

GUM TRAGACANTH

A weak solution of gum tragacanth is used in applying enamel to metals This may be bought in powdered form at any drugstore. One teaspoonful of the tragacanth is dissolved with enough pure wood alcohol in a quart jar to form a paste. Use only pure wood alcohol because isopropyl or any denatured alcohol can cause cloudiness in both opaque and transparent enamels To this paste, one quart of water is added. The solution is next shaken vigorously and allowed to stand overnight. The thin solution which rises to the top of the bottle is used as a spray in an atomizer. The thicker solution at the bottom is kept for more detailed work later. For instance, beads of enamel may be applied and held in place by this concentrated tragacanth.

Other materials and tools will be explained as they are needed in developing our first piece of enamel.

III

MAKING THE FIRST PIECE OF ENAMEL:

Shaping the copper · Trimming · Cleaning · Acid bath · Alkalizing · Washing the enamel · Applying the counterenamel · Firing the enamel · Tracing the design · Spatula method · Dusting method · Deep bowls · Warping · Blowtorch firing

FOR THE first piece of enamel, the design of which has first been worked out in color on paper, a small circular disk of pure 18-gauge copper will be used The circular disk is either spun or hammered to a slightly concave shape (*Fig* 17). Spun copper shapes may be purchased ready-made. If shaped by hand, the copper is first heated red hot and cooled by immersion in cold water. This process is called annealing. By means of this process the copper is softened enough to be hammered into the desired shape with a dogwood or rawhide mallet.

SHAPING THE COPPER

Using a rawhide mallet avoids hammer marks and is, therefore, recommended. It is advisable to work from the center of the copper out toward the circumference. A hollowed depression in a wooden block, or stake tree as it is called (*Fig.* 18), will suffice for this purpose, since it is not our aim now to create an elaborate upturned edge but merely a shallow, round tray

On more involved shapes the copper would soon become hardened after hammering and would need to be reannealed many times, but for the slight depression in the disk which we now need, a single annealing should prove sufficient.

If care is taken in hammering, a fairly smooth tray should be the result. However, for a smoother surface use the flat end of a planishing hammer, holding the tray over a suitable iron

ENAMELING: *Principles and Practice*

Fig. 17 Simple concave shapes suitable for hammering or spinning the first enameled tray.

form, such as a mushroom anvil or T stake (*Fig.* 19) This process is useful in removing any slight depressions or mounds on the surface.

TRIMMING

When the form is even (do not try for vertical sides at first, but keep the shape rather shallow), place a pair of dividers with one point at the center and the other at the circumference making a fresh mark to follow in trimming the edge. Cut off any surplus copper with metal shears and file the edge (*Fig.* 20). Whether the shape was hand-hammered or spun by lathe, the edge should be well finished before enameling. After filing the edge, which is done with a fairly fine, double-cut hand file, no further metal work on the tray is needed. We are now ready to clean the copper in preparation for the enamel.

50

Making the First Piece of Enamel

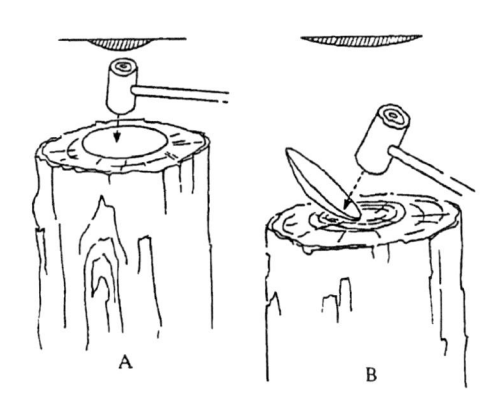

Fig. 18 Hammering in a Stake Tree   A. Start by hammering in the center of the tray   B Work out toward the edge of the tray.

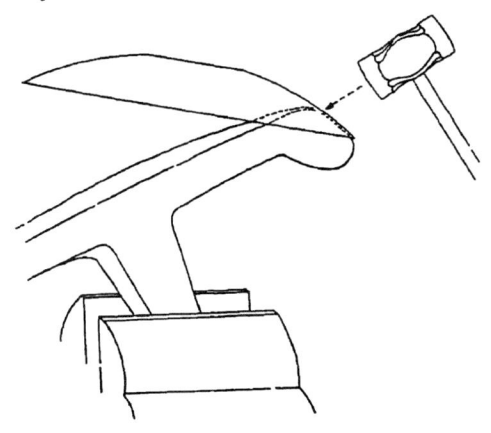

Fig. 19 Planishing over T stake. Continue each operation all around the tray The curve of the tray must fit the form of the stake.

CLEANING

The process used in cleaning the copper depends on the condition of the surface or the amount of grease which might have been deposited on it. In the case of spun pieces, there is always some wax or tallow on the surface, which was used by the spinner to prevent tool burn. This must always be thoroughly removed. To do so, place the copper tray on a block of charcoal or asbestos,

Fig 20 Trimming the edge of the tray with metal shears or tin snips. Do not try to cut with the points of the shears.

heat with a blowtorch until red and then cool (*Fig.* 21). The tray can also be placed in the kiln, heated to about 1400° F and then cooled

ACID BATH

When cool, the copper is placed in a diluted solution of nitric acid (one part pure nitric acid to three parts water, or one part commercial nitric acid to two parts water). When preparing the solution of acid and water, be sure that first the water is placed in the receptacle, preferably a Pyrex ovenware dish. Then, slowly add the nitric acid (*Fig.* 22). *Do not add water to the acid,*

Making the First Piece of Enamel

Fig. 21 Remove any grease, wax or tallow by passing the blowtorch flame over the tray.

WARNING!

Fig. 22 *Always* add the acid to the water. *Never* add water to acid.

ENAMELING: *Principles and Practice*

for this causes a violent chemical reaction and great damage will result. When the copper is a clean pink color remove it from the acid.

Rinse and dry the copper as soon as it is taken from the acid. This is done to prevent undue discoloration caused by oxidation. The brown acid fumes are dangerous to breathe and, therefore, it might be well to work in a ventilated room

ALKALIZING

To remove the stains of oxidation, polish the piece with No. 00 fine steel wool (*Fig.* 23). In order to guarantee against further acid condition on the copper, the old-fashioned method (which I still recommend) is to use saliva, which completely alkalizes the surface. It is possible to use household ammonia or any of the

Fig. 23 Polish with steel wool, using a circular motion, until a bright finish is achieved.

Making the First Piece of Enamel

Fig. 24 Wipe the surface of the tray with an alkalizing agent, such as a soapless detergent or saliva

modern soapless detergents for this purpose. A few drops of a liquid soapless detergent on a rag wiped over the surface of the copper gives excellent results. A solution of gum tragacanth about as thin as ordinary mucilage, to which a drop of the liquid detergent has been added, is more expedient when larger pieces are done (*Fig.* 24). The purpose of this final step before enameling, as previously stated, is to remove all traces of acid and of grease deposited by the steel wool. Threads from the steel wool are another hazard. If any are present when the enamel is fired, they will fuse into the enamel and cannot be removed unless stoned away with a Carborundum stone.

The test for final readiness is easily given. Simply run the copper under water and if the water does not form in beads, or

ENAMELING: *Principles and Practice*

droplets, on the surface, we are ready to go ahead with the application of enamel. Do not let the fingers touch the surface because the cleaning process will then have to be repeated to remove finger marks. Some authorities recommend placing the metal in water until ready for enameling to prevent further oxidation.

A quicker method of cleaning suitable for larger pieces is to use a commercial polishing agent known as Lea Buffing Compound. This substance will clean the copper in one step because it is a greaseless polishing agent. It is sold in the form of paste and can be applied with a cotton buff. Allow the paste to dry on the buff until stiff because it will then clean more efficiently.

WASHING THE ENAMEL

The enamel, assuming it is ground to 60 or 80 mesh, is placed in two-ounce jars and each color is washed (*Fig. 25*). Impurities and finely ground enamel dust in it necessitate washing several times. To do this, flood the enamel in a two-ounce jar with water,

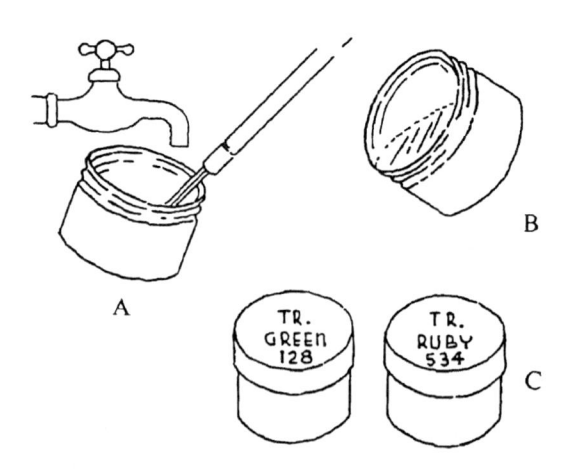

Fig. 25 Washing the Enamel A. Flush with running water while constantly stirring with the spatula B. Pour off any milky precipitate C. Label each color and place in two-ounce jars ready for enameling.

Making the First Piece of Enamel

rinse and, after it settles, pour away the excess water and impurities precipitated, leaving the enamel damp and ready for use

The opaque enamels need only one washing to remove any foreign matter, but the transparent colors become much brighter and clearer when washed several times. It is well to have two small glasses and a syringe (*Fig.* 26) handy to wash the enamels each time they are used. Label each color carefully so as to avoid later confusion of similarly colored unfired enamels

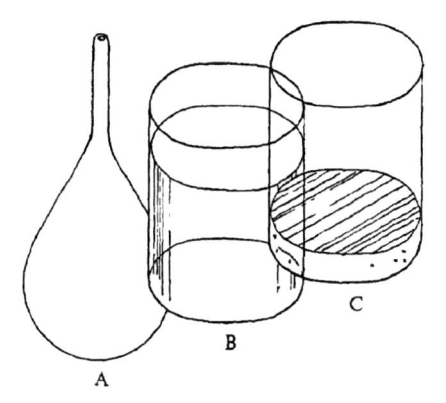

Fig. 26 A. Rubber syringe for flushing the enamels while in jars B One glass is used for clean water C One glass is for waste water and scrap enamel.

APPLYING THE COUNTERENAMEL

Place the tray upside down on a small block of wood or box cover which will enable you to turn it easily. Then apply a coat of any color enamel about $\frac{1}{32}$ inch thick to this convex (bottom) surface Use either the dusting or spatular method explained later in the chapter Leave a small area in the center, about the size of a fifty-cent piece, unenameled. If you are using a transparent color, apply it as thinly as possible, but for the opaques a little heavier coat gives a better result.

This backing enamel is known as counterenamel (*Fig.* 27) and is necessary to control the chipping or cracking caused by the

ENAMELING. *Principles and Practice*

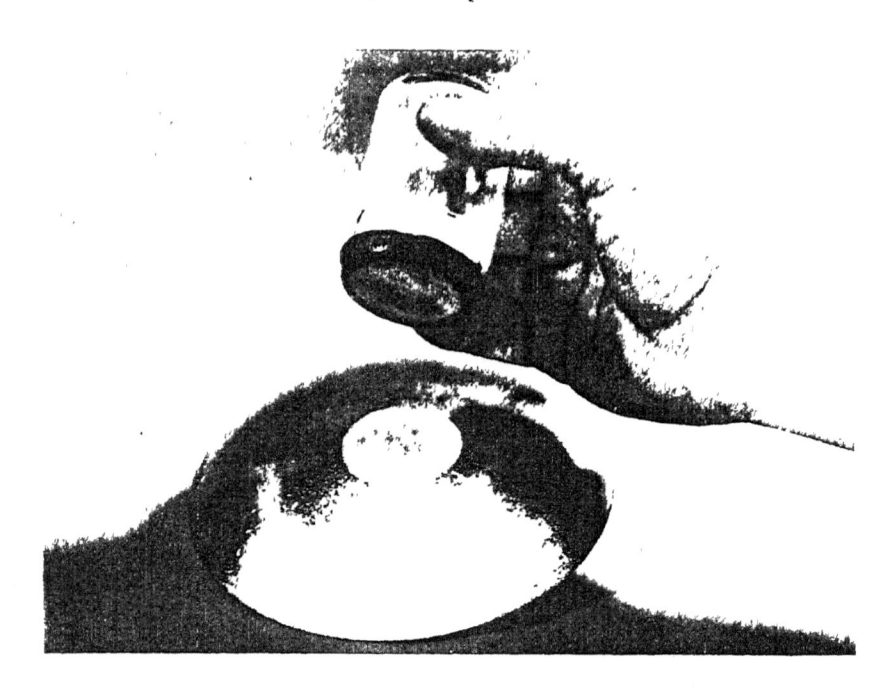

Fig 27 Here the back of the tray was counterenameled by the dusting method A disk of absorbent paper was placed in the center and then removed before firing.

difference in the rates of expansion and contraction of the copper and enamel For enameling on a concave surface such as an ash tray the counterenamel may be omitted, and the copper left exposed and later polished, but for a convex surface such as a setting for a brooch or even a flat surface like a picture the counterenamel is always used as a safeguard against cracking. The contraction of the metal when cooling after the enamel has been fused must be synchronized with the contraction of the cooling enamel or the glaze will remain in position as the metal shrinks away from it Counterenamel is one way to prevent crackling, surface textures and imperfections.

While working with the damp enamels from the jars, one should keep the piece constantly wet by spraying it with a weak solution of tragacanth. The secret of laying on the enamel rapidly

Making the First Piece of Enamel

and evenly is to keep it at just the right degree of moistness. If too wet, the enamel is uncontrollable, but if wet to the saturation point and no more, you will find that with practice you gain speed and efficiency.

Push the enamel well out to the edges and keep the unenameled area in the center free from enamel grains. With an atomizer—an ordinary nose-and-throat sprayer will do—give the piece one final application of diluted tragacanth (*Fig.* 28). You will find that as this gum solution dries, tiny particles of enamel are held in place firmly, which is a great help when transferring the piece to the kiln and aids in allowing the particles to fuse into a homogeneous layer.

The enamel *must be* completely dry before it is placed in the hot kiln. If there is much moisture in the enamel the sudden evaporation will cause vigorous steaming. Either dry the piece

Fig. 28 Spray gum tragacanth with the atomizer. Keep enamel wet to the saturation point.

ENAMELING: *Principles and Practice*

by placing it over a low heat or hold it near the door of the kiln for a few minutes Be certain that there is no steam coming from the piece before it is placed inside the kiln

FIRING THE ENAMEL

We are now ready to place the piece in the kiln for fusing the counterenamel. There are several methods of doing this (*Fig.* 29), but I will describe two of the simplest methods.

Method number one (*Fig* 29₅) place two blocks of high-fired clay or insulating brick on either side of the kiln floor. A third

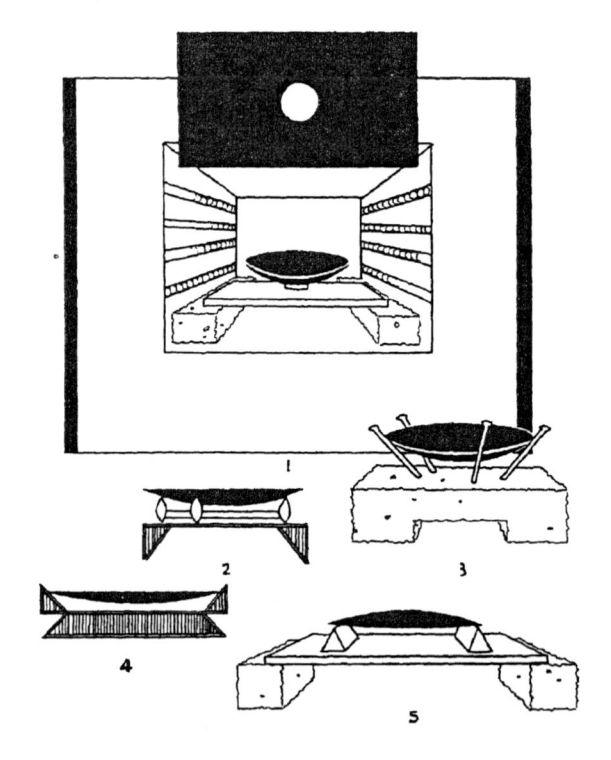

Fig 29 Methods of Placing a Circular Tray in the Kiln 1. Make a bridge of fire brick and asbestos board and place a disk of asbestos under the tray 2. Ceramic stilts and stainless steel stand 3. Ordinary steel spikes are pounded into the fire brick 4. Stainless steel stand 5. Fire brick bridge used with triangular ceramic stilts.

60

Making the First Piece of Enamel

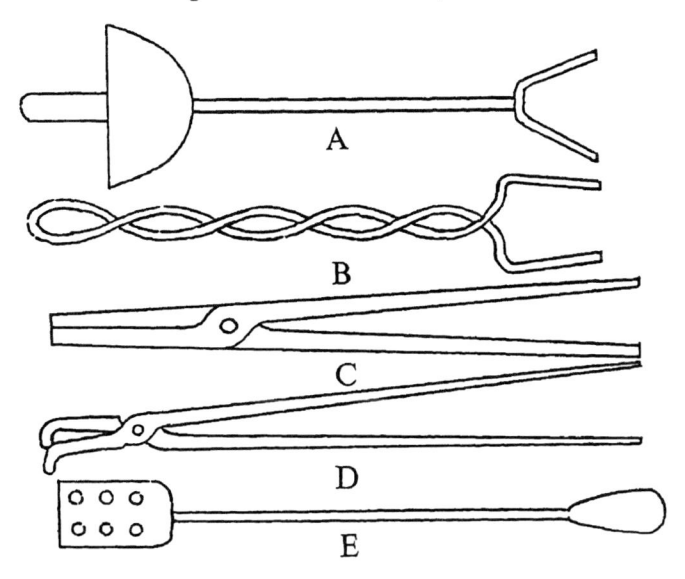

Fig 30 Tongs A. Wire tongs with plastic heat guard B. Improvised wire tongs C Forge tongs. D. Crucible tongs E. Pancake spatula.

piece of some sort of refractory board is used as a platform to straddle the two blocks in the kiln. A solid homogeneous sheet of asbestos fiber with an inorganic binder is most satisfactory for this purpose. Merely put the tray upside down on this board, lift it up with your own improvised wire tongs (*Fig.* 30B) or an ordinary kitchen spatula (*Fig.* 30E) and place it in the kiln. You may need asbestos gloves or mittens.

Method number two. procure a sheet of Monel metal, or other stainless steel which does not throw off the fire glaze when cooling. Fire glaze is oxidized metal which forms on the surface and flies off in small pieces. Cut diagonal slits at the corners of the metal sheet turning four points up and four down to form a stand For a flat tray or plate, the turned-up corners are so fitted that they just touch the outer edge of the tray and never come into contact with the enamel (*Fig.* 29₄) This method is not practical when a deep or incurved bowl is made, but does enable one to enamel the back of the tray entirely without damage to the edges. The

ENAMELING: *Principles and Practice*

Monel stand is placed in the kiln with heavy-gauge steel or copper wire tongs which can be fashioned to fit the particular size of the opening of your kiln.

The heat needed for our first small tray is from 1450° F. to 1500° F and firing it is not unlike baking cookies in an oven. Use the same amount of judgment and firing sense and, by all means, do it yourself. You alone are the one who will have to control the results Here I would suggest that you do not try to time each piece by a complicated system of arithmetic, or notations. There are many things which will occur to alter the firing time, such as soft and hard enamels, large and small pieces, various metals and metal foil, etc. A better way is to fire by what is called "The Coloration Method", in other words, to become familiar with the color in the kiln when both the enamel and the copper have reached the maximum heat.

You may be assisted by the following table when firing by coloration. Most firing is done at approximately 1470° F, which is designated in the table as a dull cherry-red.

Degrees Fahrenheit	Color
750	Red heat visible in dark
885	Red heat visible in twilight
975	Red heat visible in daylight
1080	Red heat visible in sunlight
1290	Dark red
1470	Dull cherry-red
1650	Cherry-red
1830	Bright cherry-red
2000	Orange-red

Optional accessories, such as the pyrometer which gives the correct temperature in the kiln, are usually sold separately. If you know the coloration method described above, the pyrometer is not an absolute necessity but its convenience and the peace of mind

Making the First Piece of Enamel

which it offers while firing make it a great boon to the student. As more advanced types of enameling are tried, especially work on fine gold and silver, one finds the pyrometer indispensable

The rheostat, a means of regulating the electric current by variable resistances, is another piece of equipment not absolutely essential to have. It does, however, enable the enameler to work at several jobs simultaneously and set his kiln at any given temperature. Most classrooms would find it the best means of controlling the usual crowded situation at the kiln, although the home craftsman will find the three-way switch quite satisfactory.

As enamel becomes completely fused it takes on a reddish hue not unlike burning coal The copper of the tray will also appear a rosy red, and at this point, remove the enamel from the kiln. When cooled it should present a perfectly smooth varnishlike surface with no flaws, pits, cracks or other imperfections.

As the copper cools, notice the tiny pieces of black fire glaze which fly off into the air. The enameler must be wary of these specks of fire glaze, for if they fly off from the exposed parts of copper or from another piece and rest on your enamel they immediately fire onto it and become imbedded, spoiling the effect entirely. Each time before the tray is refired, remove all such fire glaze from the unenameled copper and particularly from the copper edge by rubbing with fine emery cloth or coarse steel wool. I find that by coating the exposed copper with yellow ochre mixed with water the fire glaze is much less troublesome to remove.

We are now ready to work on the face, or concave, side of the tray. First clean the face by the same procedure as the back, with one exception Do not place the entire piece in the acid bath. It may cause damage to your counterenamel. To do this, improvise a small applicator or swab (*Fig.* 31) by wrapping a strip of rag around a wooden dowel. Holding the tray with metal tongs apply the acid with the swab and wash immediately in cold water.

TRACING THE DESIGN

If a pattern of several colors is intended, the tracing or direct

ENAMELING: *Principles and Practice*

Fig. 31 Use a swab for cleaning the front of a tray with acid When the tray is held in this position the acid does not touch the counterenamel.

pencil drawing is made on the copper (*Fig.* 32). With the pointer or jeweler's scribe make a lightly incised line over the pencil line. This should be done before the final acid bath is given in order to remove any carbon deposited by pencil lead or tracing paper A row of small bubbles will form wherever the carbon is left on the copper The design is applied in the same manner as the solid color of the counterenamel, except that one color must be juxtaposed against the next. The matter of perfecting the joining of the color areas is again something which takes a bit of practice.

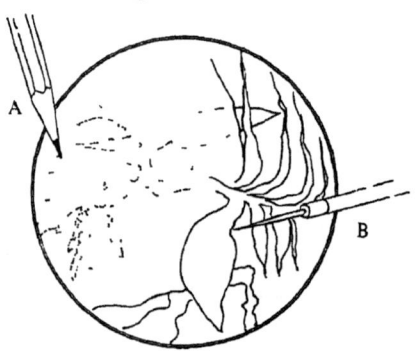

Fig. 32 Tracing   A. Draw on the copper with a pencil   B. Scratch the line with a scriber and remove pencil lines with acid.

64

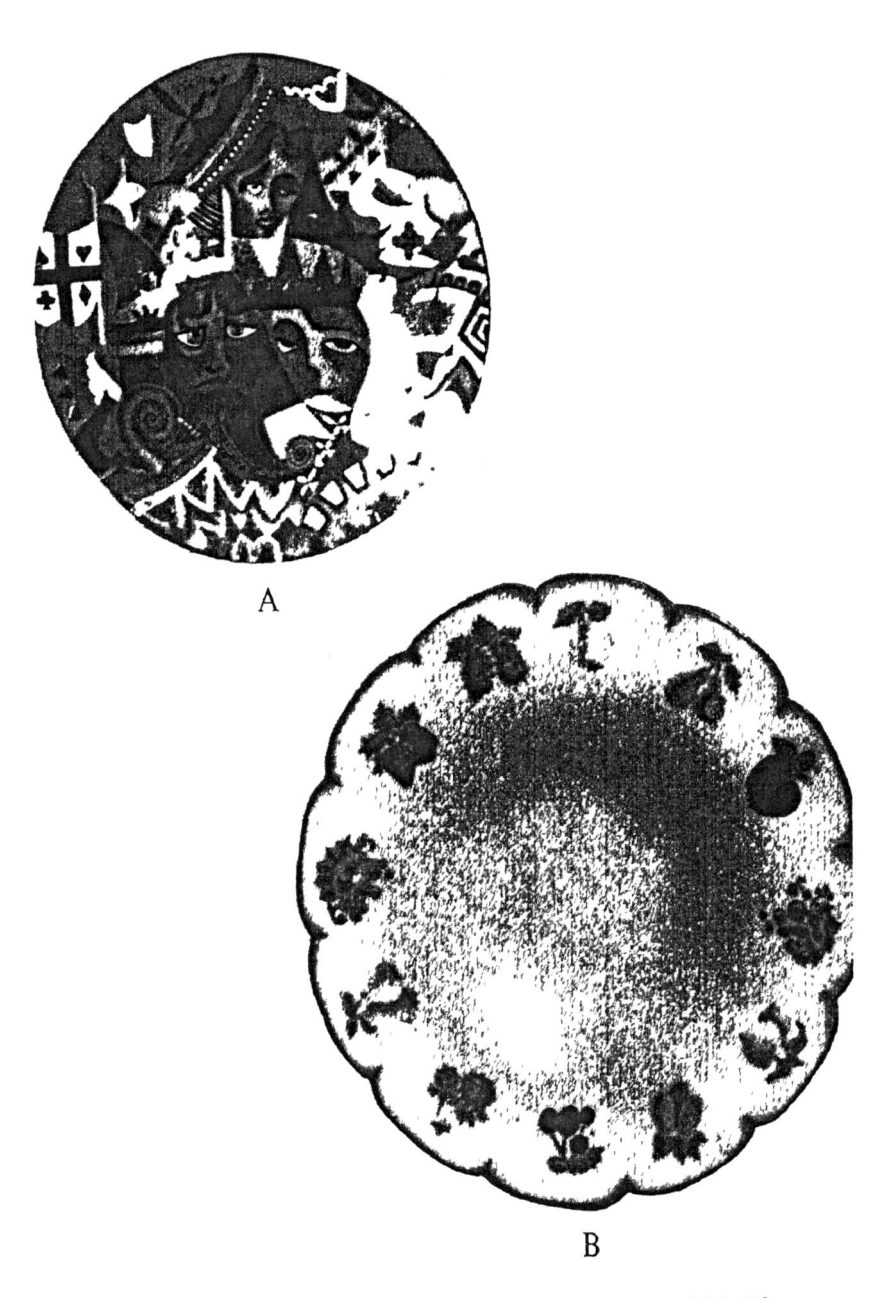

Fig. 39 (Top) A. *The Royal Family*, KENNETH F. BATES, 1946. The separate colors are inlaid, or set into, the design *(Courtesy Contemporary American Ceramic Collection, Syracuse Museum)* *(Bottom)* B. *Fruits of My Orchard*, KENNETH F. BATES, 1943. Overglaze painting in the Limoges manner.

Making the First Piece of Enamel

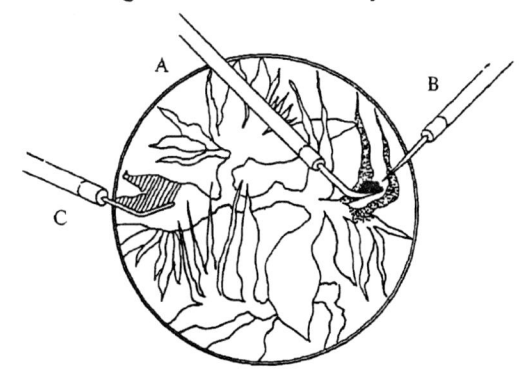

Fig. 33 Spatula Method A Hold the enamel with the spatula B Push enamel in place with the pointer C Level off enamel with the spreader.

SPATULA METHOD

Complete the first area of color, level it off carefully with the spreader and start the color area next to it (*Fig.* 33). Now with this color also wet to the saturation point, but not flowing, merely join up the two areas. With two opaque colors, such as black and white, the joining edge must be perfect. A small sable brush is sometimes used to facilitate this process.

The small circular area left on the bottom of the tray now comes into use, for if the bottom were to be placed on the asbestos or fire brick in firing the face of the tray, the enamel would adhere and ruin the underside. Cut a disk of asbestos board slightly smaller than the unenameled area on the base and use this as a stand for the tray when firing the top side (*Fig.* 29). Less easy to use are the small tripods of clay sold for ceramic work, called refractory stilts (*Fig.* 34 B and C), or you may make your own by bending up a piece of Monel metal in the form of a tripod (*Fig.* 34 A and D). The tray has a tendency to slide off to the side when it is placed in the kiln on a tripod and, in addition, leaves three tiny blemishes on the base of the tray similar to those seen on most dinnerware.

If each step has been carefully followed, your enameled tray

ENAMELING: *Principles and Practice*

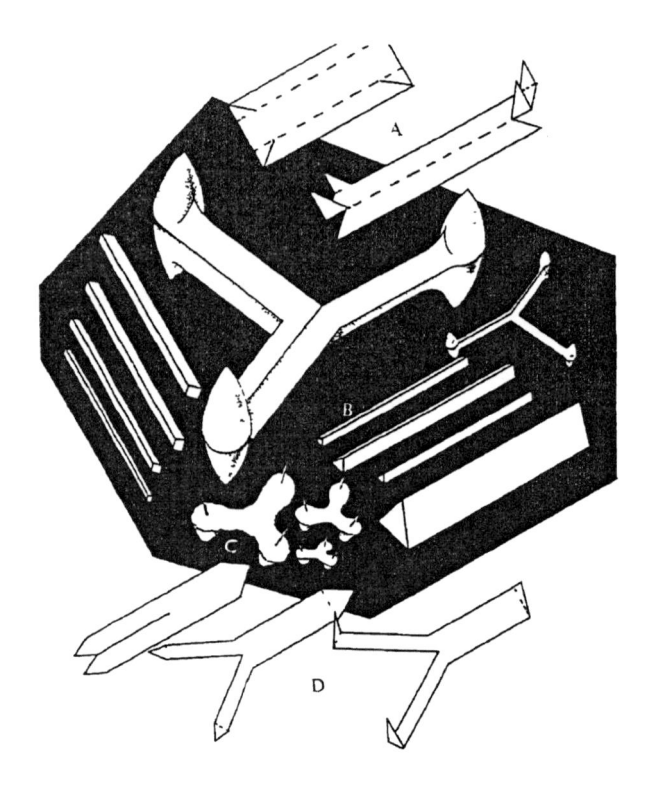

Fig. 34 Stilts and Stands for Firing   A Stainless steel stand showing plan for making one   B Refractory or ceramic stilts   C. Refractory or ceramic stilts with stainless steel pins   D. A stilt from one straight piece of metal

should begin to show some promise at this stage, although there are many colors which are more effective after a second coat is fired. You may find that the softer opaque colors, those which fuse at a lower temperature, are not an even color but show darkened areas. This is where the colors have burned out. Also, you may have a series of bubbles in the enameled areas. Take your pointer and pierce each of these bubbles Now you are ready to repeat the process by enameling the same design directly over the first one. This is not always necessary, but it is one way to achieve better final results.

Making the First Piece of Enamel

When all of your discrepancies, blemishes, poor edges, bubbles, pits and burned-out areas are remedied. file and polish the edges and the small copper area on the back You have now created your first piece of enamel (*Fig* 35), and you alone may sign your name on the back

For the first piece of enamel we might have used an entirely different approach. The method just described, called "spatula" or "inlaid" method of enameling, has enabled us to place either opaque or transparent colors in juxtaposition directly on the copper. The second method which I will now describe has its limitations, but it is actually quicker

Fig. 35 *Bird of Paradise Flower*, KENNETH F. BATES, 1943. An example of the spatula, or inlaid method.

ENAMELING: *Principles and Practice*

DUSTING METHOD

This we will call the "sifting" or "dusting" method, using dry enamel Again, a fairly flat-shaped tray must be used. On vertical surfaces the dry enamel has a tendency to drop off the copper In this case, we will enamel first the face, or concave side The copper is cleaned in the method described above and placed on a small wood block over a piece of clean white paper After the enamel is washed carefully, it is dried over a flame or hot plate It is then sifted through a fine mesh wire over the copper surface and fired. Most hardware stores carry pieces of copper wire screening of 100 mesh or finer Remove the cover from a small bottle and stretch this fine mesh wire over it (*Fig* 36A) or improvise a small basket of the wire by bending up its sides (*Fig.* 36B) The secret of the shaking method is the mesh of the screen. If the grains of enamel are fine enough they tend to fuse together, whereas grains at 60 mesh will give a spotty effect For firing this tray use the Monel metal or stainless steel platform previously described (*Fig.* 29₄), placing the tray so that the very edges of the circumference are touched by the platform. The underside can be enameled in the same way after removing the fire glaze caused in the first firing

Very nice effects can be achieved by dusting several colors together, particularly around the edge, before putting the piece

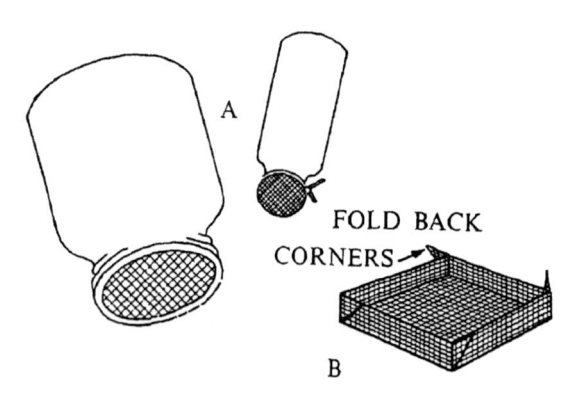

Fig. 36 Dusting Method   A. Dusting bottles   B. Wire mesh basket for dusting.

Making the First Piece of Enamel

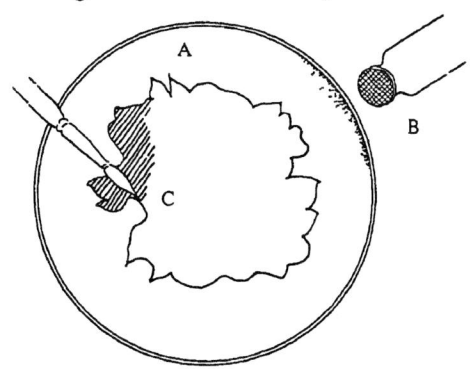

Fig. 37 Dusting Method A Background color B. Dust another enamel over first at the edge C Remove areas with a brush.

into the kiln for the first firing (*Fig.* 37B). By firing the solid color first and then applying colors dusted on for the second firing, the texture will be entirely different. A pattern or motif can be added by cutting away certain areas with a sable brush (*Fig* 37C) and filling by spatula method or by the use of metal foils and metallic lines as described in Chapters II and III

Another way of applying a design is to first fire a solid color on the copper and then dust dry enamel over a stencil. Cut a stencil by tracing your pencil drawing onto ordinary paper toweling. Place your paper stencil on the tray, keeping it wet with the tragacanth solution and dust the exposed area with dry enamel. Small tweezers will easily remove the paper after stenciling the pattern and the piece is ready for firing As many stencil firings as desired can be made (*Fig.* 38).

Personally, I feel that this method produces at best a rather stiff and commercial effect, mainly because each new color appears to be raised on the surface rather than set in as produced by the inlaid or spatula method (*Fig.* 39A) True enameling achieves the quality of a highly polished, smooth surface resembling that of a precious stone. The stencil process is an expedient which will not easily produce such a jewel-like effect, but has great value in larger pieces. It is certainly a method which has a future inasmuch as these raised areas can be purposely exaggerated to achieve unusual, modern effects.

ENAMELING: *Principles and Practice*

Fig. 38 *Strelitzia*, KENNETH F BATES, 1948. This is an example of the stencil method of enameling The whole composition was built up in successive stencils from a light background.

DEEP BOWLS

On deeper bowls it is quite possible to combine the dusting method with the wet method. In this case, sift only one area of the bowl at a time, working from the edge towards the center (*Fig.* 40). Eventually keep the whole bowl wet to the extreme saturation point, but be careful that the enamel does not flow.

70

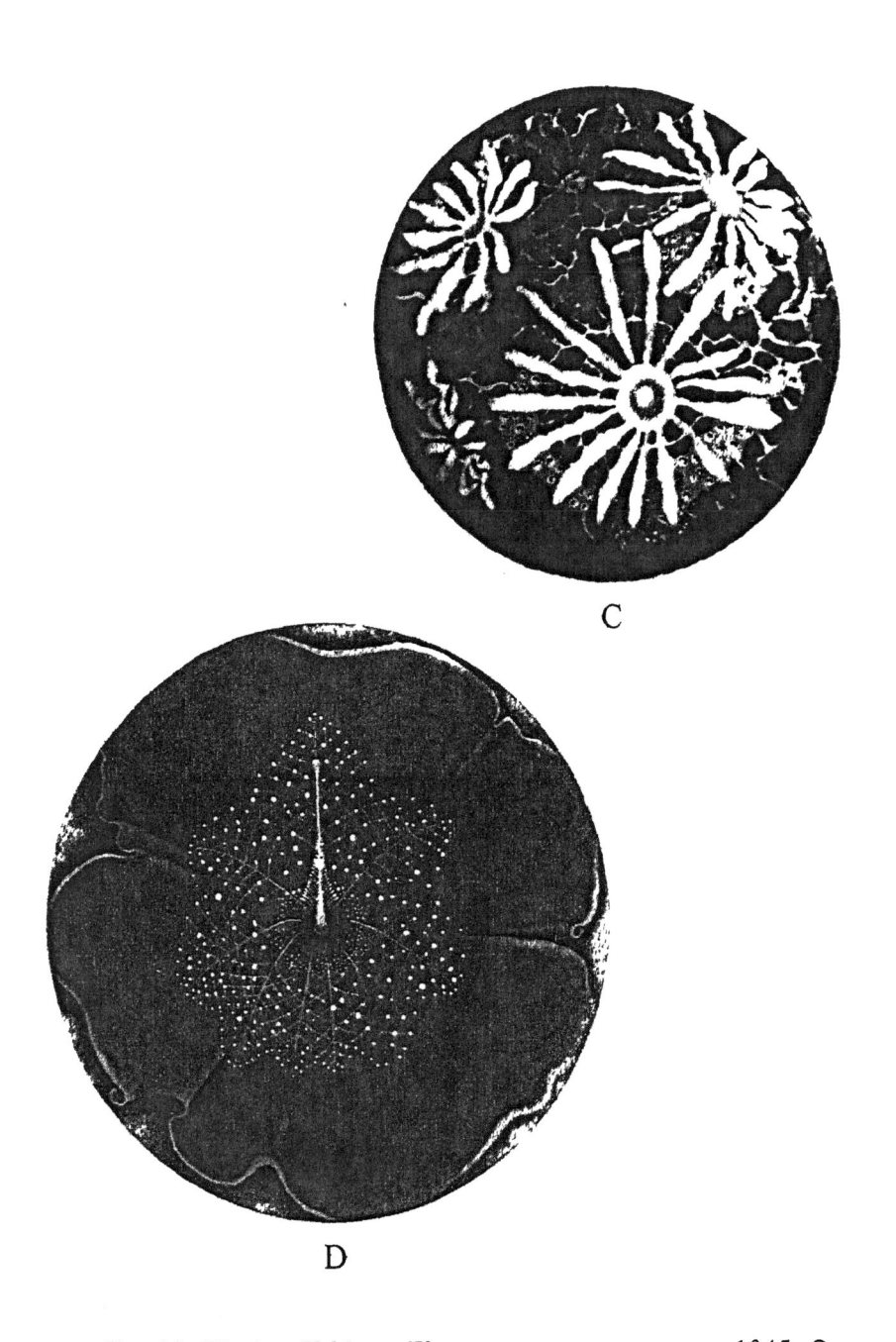

Fig. 39 *(Top)* C *Hibiscus Flower,* KENNETH F. BATES, 1945. One large-scale motif may occupy the entire area of the circle *(Bottom)* D. *Experiment 9B,* KENNETH F. BATES, 1940. In this case intentional overfiring caused the petals in the flower forms to become distorted.

Making the First Piece of Enamel

You will need at least four applications of enamel and tragacanth before your first firing in order to avoid pits or burned-out areas.

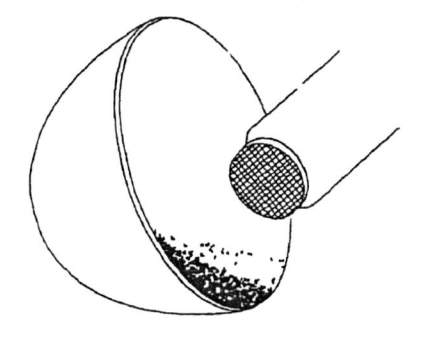

Fig 40 In a deep bowl shape completely finish one area at a time

WARPING

The problem of warping, as the pieces are fired again and again, is one which must be guarded against if the results are to be professional in appearance Using asbestos gloves, one may bend the plate while still hot, but there may be some unevenness when the final firing is accomplished

The most effective method is to turn the bowl or plate upside down immediately after it comes from the kiln, place it on a large flat piece of asbestos board and then use a heavy weight on top of it. There is nothing better than an old-fashioned flatiron, if one is fortunate enough to have one. Allow the bowl to cool with the flatiron on it (*Fig.* 41). This will assure a perfectly round form and an even circumference.

BLOWTORCH FIRING

Old books on enameling and craftwork give some importance to the use of the blowtorch for fusing the enamels. In these days when electricity is so readily available, the electric kiln should be considered an essential part of your equipment. However, there are times when a blowtorch or Bunsen burner can be used suc-

ENAMELING: *Principles and Practice*

Fig. 41 Place the bowl or plate, immediately after removing from the kiln, on a flat surface and put an old-fashioned flatiron on top of it This will correct any warping of the enameled piece

cessfully; for example, in firing a small button earring or in making a quick test. The only equipment needed is a small, square piece of iron wire screening and some sort of tripod or stand upon which to place it. The screening should be coated with loam, which will prevent any iron oxide scales from flying onto the enamel while fusing. The flame is played from beneath and must be kept from touching the surface of the enamel. Use only the blue flame, making sure that the wire screening tends to diffuse or spread the flame. In my own studio I have improvised a crude, but functional, way of firing with the blowtorch (*Fig.* 42). I place a tin can, about four inches in diameter and five inches high, on a piece of asbestos. An opening is cut in the can for the blowtorch. On the can I place the iron wire screening and then the small enamel or test piece. Over this is placed another tin can with an opening for viewing the work. In other words, an efficient and useful miniature muffled furnace has been approximated.

For large-scale production or for more rapid enameling, both

Making the First Piece of Enamel

sides of the tray may be fired at the same time. Many simple inventions can be created by the individual craftsman to expedite his work. In fact, every craftsman I know has his trade secrets and studio inventions. Some craftsmen use what is commercially sold as "glass enamel," a finely ground enamel suspended in a volatile oil or readily vaporizable vehicle, which can be quickly sprayed on both surfaces. The trays are then stacked to dry in a special drying kiln or simply in a warm room overnight. This particular type of finely ground enamel is not damaged by handling and makes a satisfactory undercoat for further colors. It should not be expected to give the same richness and depth of color that the more carefully built-up, hand-washed enamels will give. When firing the trays, both back and front at the same time, a platform of fire brick is arranged. Stainless steel pegs are driven into it at an angle so that the tray touches only at the circumference (*Fig.* 29₃).

Fig. 42 Improvise a miniature muffled furnace from tin cans when firing enamels with a blowtorch.

IV

TESTING THE COLORS, THE USE OF METAL FOILS AND THE INDIVIDUAL PALETTE:
Opaque tests · Metal foils · Transparent tests on copper · Transparent tests on pure silver · Enameling on sterling silver · Test for melting point · Palette

Now THAT the first piece has been completed, it should be quite evident that enamels behave differently when placed over other enamels They also change considerably in color when fired over different metals This change is noticeable only in the transparent or translucent colors.

The painter in oils or water colors has the opportunity of mixing several pigments on his palette before applying them to his painting, but the enamelist knows the values and hues of colors only after his glazes have matured in the kiln.

Because it is quite impossible to match colors and close values before firing, the only solution is to make individual tests which will show at a glance what can be expected of each color after it is fired. As the work progresses and more elaborate juxtapositions of transparent and opaque colors are called for by the composition, these tests are absolutely indispensable. Otherwise the superficial attraction for the bright, sparkling colors may lead one into hackneyed color schemes of little aesthetic value. The more seriously the matter of making tests is taken and the more thoroughly it is done, the greater scope the enamelist will have for his future experimentations in color and composition.

These test colors may be kept in a box or strung onto a loop of wire, so they may be used in deciding color schemes. It is even better to hang them on a plaque or chart with small hooks where they are always before you for reference. By placing a number of

Testing Colors, Use of Metal Foils, the Individual Palette

tests near each other you will readily see a variety of possible color combinations

One should work out three types of tests Each of the opaques needs to be tested over copper (or, in some cases, over an opaque white) to determine its effects. Each transparent should be tested over the metal foils and fluxes to show all of its possible color changes, and also over pure silver

OPAQUE TESTS

The opaque tests (*Fig.* 43) need space for only two variations of the color. Bend a one-inch square tab of copper in a shallow arc, file its edges, drill a hole at the top for hanging, and prepare for enameling. Apply the counterenamel and fire. The arc-shaped

TEST FOR TRANSPARENT ENAMELS

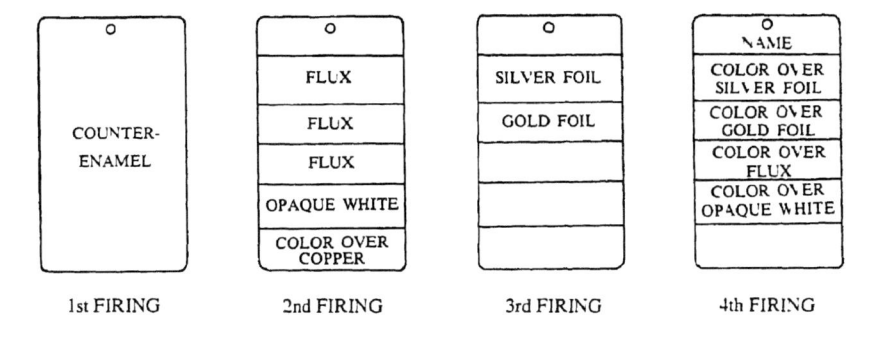

COUNTER-ENAMEL	FLUX / FLUX / FLUX / OPAQUE WHITE / COLOR OVER COPPER	SILVER FOIL / GOLD FOIL	NAME / COLOR OVER SILVER FOIL / COLOR OVER GOLD FOIL / COLOR OVER FLUX / COLOR OVER OPAQUE WHITE
1st FIRING	2nd FIRING	3rd FIRING	4th FIRING

TEST FOR OPAQUE ENAMELS

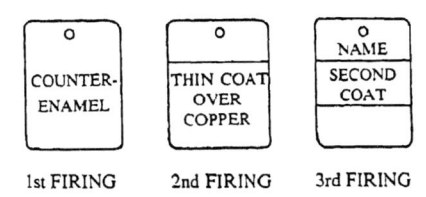

COUNTER-ENAMEL	THIN COAT OVER COPPER	NAME / SECOND COAT
1st FIRING	2nd FIRING	3rd FIRING

Fig 43 Diagram showing steps in firing the transparent and opaque enamel tests.

ENAMELING: *Principles and Practice*

tab will serve two purposes. one, the enamel never touches the kiln except at the very edge of the counterenamel; and, two, it is easily lifted with a small spatula or ordinary kitchen knife.

The front side of the test is now cleaned and prepared for enameling. Place the opaque enamel over the entire front surface. For experimentation, give the opaque an overfiring. By overfiring we mean raising the temperature to a heat above that which is needed to actually mature or fuse the glass In the case of the average opaque enamel this would be about 1650° F., or even higher with some yellows and beige If your opaque is a soft color, it may fuse as low as 1200° F. The harder the color, the higher the temperature is a good point to remember. Also keep in mind that it is not only the temperature to which the enamel is brought nor the length of time it is in the kiln, but a combination of these two factors. In other words, a hard enamel kept in the kiln for a long period at a low heat would not give the same results as subjecting it to a high heat for a shorter time.

In overfiring the opaque enamel on your test you will find that often there will be darkened areas, as in the case of red and vermilion. Other colors will become distinctly transparent. Leave one-half of the tab in the overfired condition for your palette of effects and apply another, slightly thicker, coat of opaque to the remaining half Fire at a lower temperature than before (about 1450° F) and you will have as a result a complete test of one opaque color, showing it in both its true and its overfired state. The true opaque color can also be achieved by firing the second coat over an opaque white, so long as the white is not a softer color than the other opaque. The soft white shows through in spots and, while an interesting effect is gained, it is not a true representation of the color.

METAL FOILS

With copper, which is, after all, the metal most generally used in enameling, it is possible to attain the same colors as those over pure silver without actually enameling on heavy-gauge silver but on silver foil. Both silver and gold foil can be bought in

Testing Colors, Use of Metal Foils, the Individual Palette

booklets containing twelve or more sheets each approximately four inches square. Do not mistake the ordinary gold or silver leaf used by window decorators in lettering on glass, for the foil used in enameling. The foil enamelists use is fifteen times heavier in weight and also pure metal. The silver foil is known as non-adhesive No 4 and called by some companies "cutch" silver. The areas of silver foil used in the Limoges type of enameling are labeled "paillons" and will be spoken of as such in this book.

Now prepare a piece of copper ¾ inch wide by 1½ inches long for the transparent tests. Any one of the transparents is first fired over this copper tab in a smooth coat. If bubbles occur in this firing they should be patched by first pricking them open with the steel pointer and then rubbing grains of the same color into these tiny pits before refiring. Now the shape of the paillon is traced onto a piece of tracing paper and the silver foil is held between it and another piece of tracing paper, then cut with sharp shears or a razor blade. The paillon is next punched with many pinpoints (*Fig.* 44), preferably 150 to 200 per square inch, so as to allow air to escape from under the foil when it is fused to the enamel On smaller paillons this process can be eliminated. The process is greatly simplified if a dozen or more needles are thrust through a large cork, allowing the points to project about ¼ inch from the cork. Proceed to prick the surface of the silver paillon.

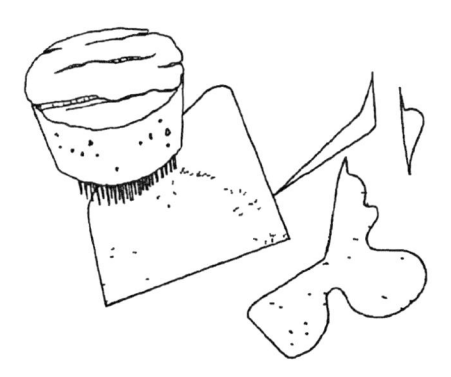

Fig. 44 Holes are punched in the silver paillons at the rate of 100 per square inch.

ENAMELING: *Principles and Practice*

Adhere the paillon to the enameled surface with gum tragacanth solution and carefully absorb any excess moisture with a blotter or soft rag. It is difficult to say just how long the silver or gold foil should be fired. When it is completely adhered to the enamel it is fired sufficiently. Take it out of the kiln during the process of firing and burnish it with the back of a dull kitchen knife or artist's spatula (*Fig* 45). Caution should be taken not to overfire the paillon as it is quite possible to burn it, in which case it is ruined and will have to be stoned off with a Carborundum stick.

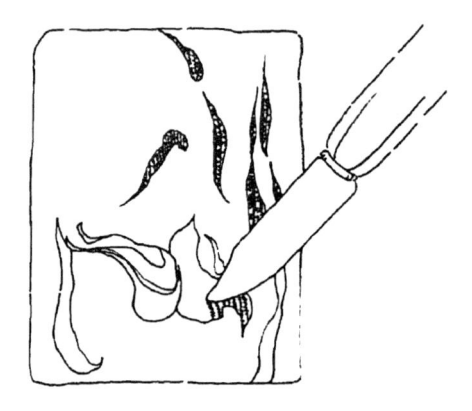

Fig 45 Burnish the silver paillons with a dull kitchen knife and return to the kiln until adhered to the enamel.

TRANSPARENT TESTS ON COPPER

Making transparent tests on copper involves four separate firings (*Fig.* 43).

Firing No. 1, or the counterenamel firing, should not be left in the kiln too long because with the high temperature, fire glaze becomes heavily imbedded on the upper side of the test piece and is difficult to remove. Give just enough firing to set the counterenamel as it will be fused further in the subsequent firings. After cleaning the front surface, prepare to show the transparent color as it looks over silver foil, gold foil, flux, opaque white and copper. This will involve three separate firings.

Testing Colors, Use of Metal Foils, the Individual Palette

Firing No. 2 has the color applied directly over copper for the area at the bottom At the same time an area of opaque white and three areas of flux are placed above. Fire, clean the edges with file or emery cloth and wipe off the surface in preparation for the next step.

Firing No 3 enables us to place the silver paillon and the gold paillon over two of the flux areas in the manner described above Fire as before, being sure that the paillons are burnished down so that they adhere perfectly to the enamel (*Fig.* 45).

Clean and proceed to Firing No. 4, which is the last firing, giving us the color effect over opaque white, flux, gold, and silver An additional firing may still be made if metallic paint is used for labeling each test. The number, name and type of enamel should be clearly marked at the top of the test piece

TRANSPARENT TESTS ON PURE SILVER

In making tests of the transparents on pure silver, there are a few processes which differ from those used on copper To clean fine silver, first heat the small piece to be used to a dull-red color and cool. It must now be pickled in a diluted sulfuric acid solution (instead of in nitric acid), approximately one part sulfuric acid to four parts water. The pickle must be hot, but not boiling, and a Pyrex container is necessary for use over the flame. Leave the silver in the solution until it is a clean, whitish color. After pickling, rinse the silver and give it a quick dip in warm nitric acid, one part acid to one part water, and rinse again. This bright dip gives a whiter appearance to the silver Some authorities recommend this as the final surface for enameling on silver, but a further polish can be brought out with fine steel wool. The glass brush (*Fig* 46) may be substituted for the steel wool and gives an excellent finish to silver. This is a bunch of glass fibers bound together with cord and is obtainable from most ceramic companies.

When applying transparent enamels to fine silver, remember that the intrinsic value of the metal is worthy of the most meticulous workmanship; therefore, the thorough washing of transpar-

ENAMELING: *Principles and Practice*

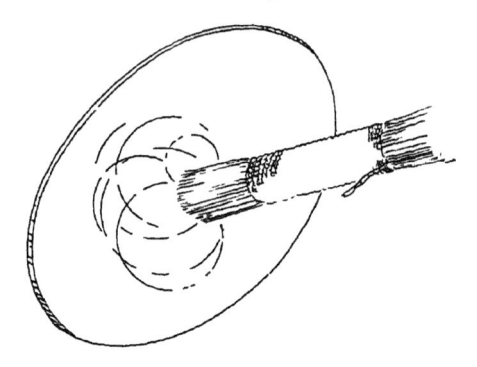

Fig 46 The glass brush should be used for a final finish on silver before enameling.

ent enamels is especially important Apply an even layer of enamel in as thin a coat as possible, not over $\frac{1}{32}$ inch thick Push the enamel out to the edges of your silver, for it has a greater tendency to recede here than on copper. If there are exposed parts or recessions at the edges, merely add more enamel and refire. No cleaning is necessary since fine silver does not oxidize in the kiln Pure silver will intensify the brilliance of your enamels. If it does not, the trouble is due to one or more of the following causes one, improper cleaning of the silver, two, improper washing of the transparent enamel; three, application of too thick a layer of enamel.

Transparent blues, greens, chartreuse, grays, lavenders and yellows are most gratifying over the fine silver. Red transparent, which gives a brilliant ruby or claret over copper, will appear orange over silver. For clear reds one must use a special red transparent enamel for silver Opaque colors will cause trouble and should not be applied in the same firing, or at least not until undercoats of transparents are first fired on the silver.

ENAMELING ON STERLING SILVER

Because sterling silver is an alloy, there is great possibility that your enameling on it may meet with failure. It contains 92½ per cent silver in combination, usually, with copper. The difficulties

Testing Colors, Use of Metal Foils, the Individual Palette

met with in my classroom have been caused not as the piece is fired for the first time, but in subsequent firings It has been observed that as the enamel cracks in each firing, the small proportion of alloy (copper or other metals) discolors the surface of the silver leaving black streaks or lines. Generally speaking, it is much safer to use fine silver for enameling and the cost is only slightly greater

There is also the problem of temperature when firing on sterling silver, inasmuch as it begins to break down after reaching 1500° F. It becomes liquid, or flowing, at 1640° F., whereas fine silver is liquid at 1761° F

Three safe rules to follow when enameling on sterling silver are. work on concave surfaces as much as possible to avoid surface tensions; restrict the number of firings to one or two; never raise the temperature above 1500° F.

The procedure for cleaning and preparing sterling silver for enameling is otherwise similar to that for fine silver as stated above.

The yellow transparents and the regular fluxes for copper always seem to become discolored after several firings on either sterling or fine silver In general, all colors are much less brilliant over sterling than over fine silver

It is hard to restrict oneself to a short list of colors which are best for silver, but here are some of my favorites—the names are those used by one manufacturer. sapphire medium, cobalt, royal, bird blue, emerald, aquamarine, shamrock, meadow green, light brown, mahogany brown, beige, golden tan, seal, chartreuse, tea rose pink, blue gray, orange, light turquoise, ruby, garnet, light maroon, claret red, gold, light yellow, medium lavender and dark purple.

TEST FOR MELTING POINT

Another kind of test may be made to determine the melting point of your different enamels. One can readily see that it would be advantageous to use enamels which melt at similar temperatures, if possible, on the same piece To make this test, place small

ENAMELING: *Principles and Practice*

blobs of several colors on a scrap of copper and use the blowtorch method of firing explained in Chapter III Have a second person watch carefully as each enamel becomes molten, making notes on the fusing time for each enamel. In this way the hardness or softness of each enamel may be discovered

PALETTE

With five variations to each of the transparents and two to each opaque, a reasonable palette for the average student of enamel might be one hundred colors. Each person working in enamels, however, soon discovers his preference for a certain palette. At this time, build up a catalogue of the types of colors you most favor.

In addition to the tests described, there are other variations that can be attained. Unusual effects are attained by admixtures when two or three enamels are ground together with a mortar and pestle Blotched colors will appear in the overfired opaques Speckled and spotty effects come with the overfiring of transparents on opaque white. By leaving the harder colors slightly underfired a rough and interesting texture results. If cool colors are preferred, make a greater number of tests with the silver paillons The warm colors are more brilliant and show up best over gold paillons.

Any one of these phases can be developed to suit the individual tastes in preparation for the work ahead. There is hardly a composition conceivable in which one would need a larger palette than this. Of course, one hundred colors appears to be an ambitious palette, but one must remember that within these colors it is necessary to include the entire spectrum and your whole scale of values from dark to light as each enamel remains a specific hue varying only slightly with different degrees of heat.

V

CHARACTERISTICS OF CERTAIN ENAMELS: Black · White · Gray · Flux · Blue · Green · Brown · Red · Purple · Chartreuse · Yellow · Ivory

NOTWITHSTANDING the fact that the craftsman will discover many individual characteristics of enamels by making his own tests, I am listing some personal discoveries which may be of help This list is by no means complete One of the main fascinations of this medium is the never-ending opportunity for experimentation, and in that respect it is similar to the art of pottery

The terms "soft" and "hard" enamels, as we explained, refer to those which will fuse at a low and a high temperature respectively. Unless specified by the manufacturer, one must discover this for oneself. Soft colors will appear to ooze into the harder ones as they are juxtaposed. Many of the softer opaques can be overfired, bringing them to a clear transparency Strangely enough, the opacity can then be brought back by a subsequent low firing. This is particularly true of opaque turquoise.

I have listed below some of the more unusual facts regarding certain enamels.

BLACK

For general purposes, dense black is the most satisfactory. It should be washed with care as any precipitate or cloudiness left tends to be quite evident when areas are patched As much as possible forego patching with black opaque because of this Unless completely re-enameled each time the layers of color are built up, you will find that the black also tends to burn out, leaving a dull, unattractive surface. Dense black is not acidproof, therefore never submit it to a strong acid bath for cleansing. Wherever the acid touches it the gloss will be sacrificed and there will remain a

ENAMELING: *Principles and Practice*

dull-gray, powdery-looking area. Opaque black is also obtainable in very soft, soft, medium and hard grades. At least three grades should be included in the enameler's palette.

WHITE

Much of the same information regarding opaque blacks might be given about the opaque whites, although there is an even greater variety of uses for white and, therefore, more types are offered by the manufacturer. The extremely hard white is known as dial or hard dial and, as the name implies, is widely used by jewelers for watch dials or whenever imperviousness to scratching is of prime importance. The hard dial opaque white can be applied in a paper-thin coat and still retain its opacity at a high temperature. The jeweler's dense white will produce a solid, spotless white under normal conditions. For silver work, a special white called "soft for silver" is advisable in order to avoid discolorations which often occur. There are interesting uses for hard white, one being that of underfiring it to produce an embossed or raised effect This experiment will be discussed further in Chapter X. If soft opaque white is thinly applied over copper, a bluish-green coloration will appear which is sometimes effective and used intentionally. The softest white, when applied as a thin line, becomes almost fluid as it fuses, giving the quality of water color on absorbent paper. This characteristic is true to some extent of other opaque colors, but it is most striking with white.

GRAY

Many types of gray are needed for enamel work because so much of enameling deals with intense and vibrating colors. Unless the palette contains a variety of neutral tones, the designer finds it difficult to balance his color combinations successfully. Such grays as French, pearl, steel and blue are all useful. All grays tend toward pitting but when filled with a few grains of enamel the patch is indiscernible. Transparent gray, whether it is light, dark or blue-gray, is one of the best colors over copper Not

Characteristics of Certain Enamels

enough of the warmth of the copper color shows through to destroy the neutral tones. On silver the transparent grays are even more interesting and, in my own opinion, are not used frequently enough.

FLUX

A great deal might be written in detail about the many kinds of flux, but, since the craftsman usually finds his own solution by experimentation. I shall mention only a few characteristics of this basic enamel. For the ground coating on copper, where other colors are to be laid over it, use the soft flux. This, or the soft fusing, is a general-purpose flux. It will usually remain in place and not bubble up through the top layers of enamel if it is applied in a thin coating. When the spotty effect of the flux coming to the surface occurs, a second layer of the color will produce a solid tone. If the enamel to be superimposed is known to be a hard one, your flux should be hard or medium. Flux on fine silver invariably causes trouble. A perfect glasslike quality is achieved in the first firing and then as the temperature is increased in subsequent firings a discouragingly dull, putty-colored surface appears. My only suggestion would be to minimize the number of firings and *never overfire when working with fine silver*. The best examples of the use of flux over various metals may be seen on the champlevé snuffboxes made in Battersea, England, in the Eighteenth Century.

Being a truly transparent color, flux has the characteristic of revealing any discoloration or flaw which might be on the metal. Tracing lines made with the scriber are apt to show as the flux recedes from them.

By enameling one area of flux at a time and deliberately allowing the copper to become oxidized, a brownish edge can be controlled around each shape. *Cinerarias* (*Fig.* 47) is an example of this. Flux will fuse directly over patches of fire glaze and is utilized for abstract effects and interesting textures.

ENAMELING: *Principles and Practice*

Fig. 47 *Cinerarias,* KENNETH F. BATES, 1938. Here the dark edges of the flower forms were created by allowing the copper to oxidize as each shape was added. (*Courtesy Cleveland Museum of Art*)

BLUE

The darker shades of opaque blue are excellent for backgrounds and counterenamel. They adhere to the metal with very little cracking or bubbling. They are permanent and the harder varieties are not affected by acid. Suggestions for the blue palette are: periwinkle (light value), blue jay or dark periwinkle (middle value) and lapis (dark value).

Few colors have as much "appeal to the public" as transparent blue. This color has predominated almost every period in the history of enamels. Of the many transparent blues, cobalt is a favorite. This is the dark, rich blue so often seen in the older pieces. For the lighter blue there is the delicate sapphire transparent and for middle values, the dark sapphire or bird blue. On the whole,

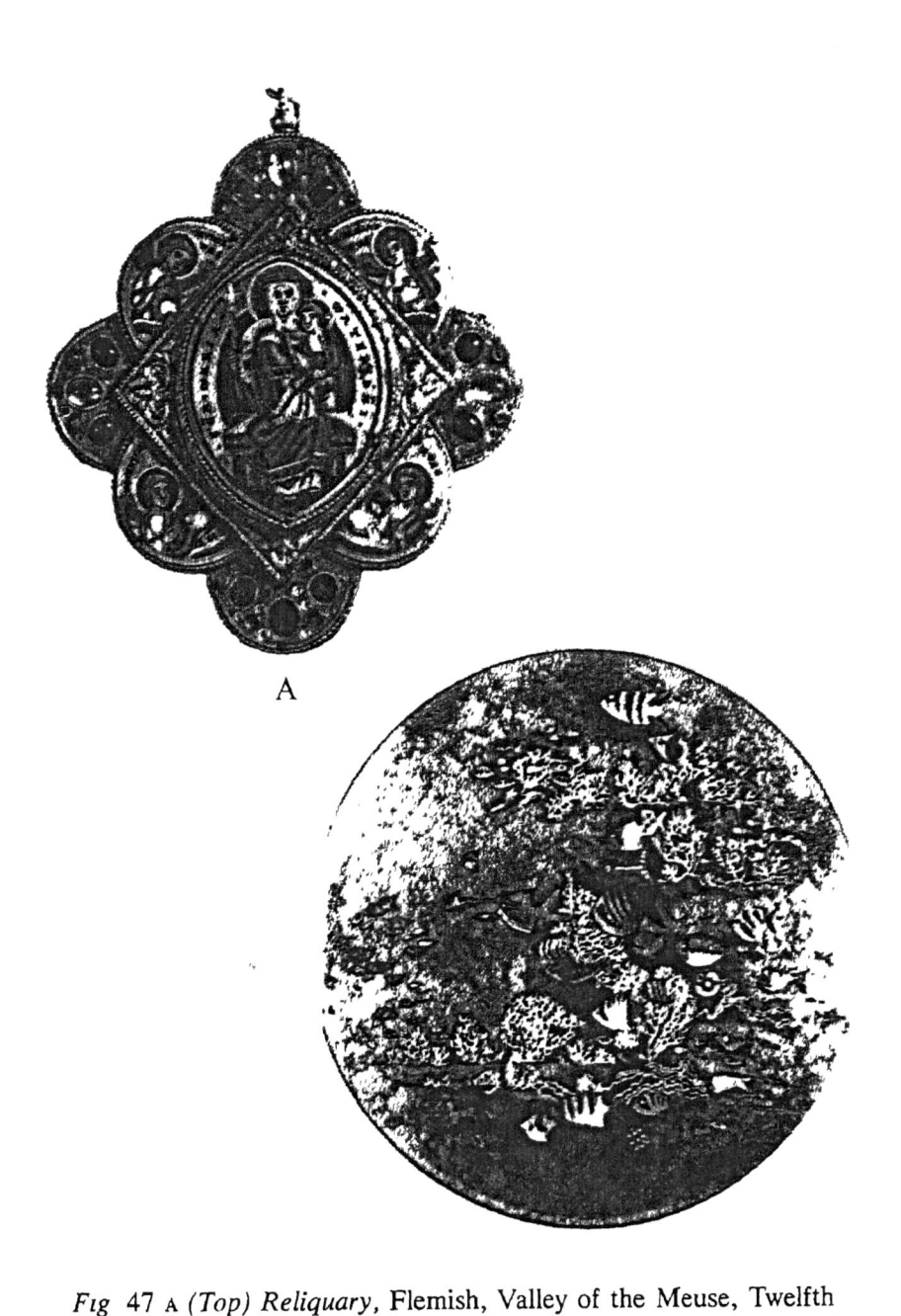

Fig 47 A *(Top) Reliquary,* Flemish, Valley of the Meuse, Twelfth Century, attributed to GODEFROID DE CLAIRE. Champlevé enamel and copper gilt *(Courtesy Cleveland Museum of Art)*
(Bottom) Ballet of Fishes, KENNETH F BATES, 1948 An example of transparent flux fired directly over patches of fire glaze to create an illusion of water in the background.

Characteristics of Certain Enamels

blue is the easiest of all colors to use, but one caution should be given concerning it in the transparent state: too thin applications will not give good results when working on copper. This is understandable when one realizes that copper, a warm-colored metal, is complementary to the blues and tends to neutralize them Therefore, it is a good plan to apply the first coat of transparent blue a bit heavier than one would other transparent colors The transparent blues are consequently ideal on silver, a cold-colored metal.

GREEN

To some extent, the transparent greens are also affected by the warm tone of copper and should be handled the same as the blues There are special transparent greens for silver, but the greens for copper, such as shamrock and emerald, are sufficiently brilliant on silver Opaque greens are inclined to be troublesome. The softer ones show pits and bubbles more often than most opaque enamels. Opaque blue-greens are subject to color changes under varying temperatures, which can be anticipated by careful notations of test firing.

BROWN

All the transparent browns and tans are stable in their color retention. Very rich browns are available, such as champagne, dark tobacco, beige and golden, and in the opaque colors one may use parchment, light tan and chocolate, to name only a few. Both transparent and opaque beige are highly recommended. As a transparent color, it gives a pinkish-tan effect over copper and is not likely to cause trouble of any kind. The opaque beige is a very hard color so that it can be left in the unfired stage while other, softer enamels are matured, thus giving a raised surface texture.

RED

Both transparent and opaque red enamels seem to be more problematic than most other colors. Being colored by the oxide of

ENAMELING. *Principles and Practice*

gold, the red enamels are exceedingly soft and tend to burn out or become fugitive Opaque reds, vermilions and oranges will disappear in high temperatures and require a second or third coat. To avoid it in the first firing is quite impossible. I suggest one coat of soft opaque white and two coats of opaque red or vermilion if a clear color is wanted.

Since red is such a soft color, it is necessary to be scrupulously careful in regard to foreign matter which might get into it A tiny particle of dust, fire glaze or undesirable enamel quickly imbeds itself in the red opaque as it is fired. This can be removed only by stoning it away with Carborundum stone or a Carborundum point on a mechanical hand tool.

An idiosyncrasy of opaque red is the black edge which it creates next to another enamel Sometimes this is very effective and can be used to advantage for decorative purposes.

There are Princeton, mikado and buccaneer oranges, and Chinese, cardinal, Navajo and Turkey reds. Being very brilliant, they should be used sparingly as they tend to "jump out" in a color composition, particularly when in solid unbroken areas.

Transparent red over copper is not usually obtained in one application In fact, the first firing of such transparent reds as ruby, claret or wine will be disappointingly dark and cloudy. A special preparation of the copper according to an old recipe should give better results. Anneal the copper to a dull red. Cool and place in a nitric acid pickle, consisting of one part nitric acid and twelve parts water After boiling in the pickle, give the copper a "bright dip." The bright dip, which, incidentally, is recommended by some for other enamels as well, is composed of equal parts of sulfuric and nitric acids with a little hydrochloric acid or a pinch of salt added. The solution should be allowed to cool before using Thoroughly rinse in clean water until all acid is removed, after which heat to an iridescent color and proceed with the regular steel-wool and alkalizing process as previously described.

More common practice is to apply red transparent enamels over a coat of flux. First fire an even, thin coat of soft fusing flux, bringing it to the pinkish-tan stage, about 1475° F. If the result is absolutely clear and transparent, proceed with the red. The

Characteristics of Certain Enamels

spatula method of application guarantees a brighter color than shaking or dusting, because the red transparent can be more thoroughly washed Lay the first coat of red over the flux, fire at 1495° F and apply the second, keeping each about $\frac{1}{32}$ inch thick. Bring the third firing to the highest heat (1500° F) and the result should be comparable to the color of a glass of red wine when held to the light or the red seen in old stained-glass windows.

If you are fortunate enough to be working on pure gold. by all means make the most of transparent reds. Although the same color quality can be obtained over gold-foil paillons, one must expect the unavoidable crinkly effect. I have found that gilding metal, which is an alloy of 90 per cent copper and 10 per cent zinc, or 95 per cent copper and 5 per cent zinc, will produce a beautiful red or pink transparent in the first firing The trouble lies in the fact that few enamels are done in one firing. and as the alloy starts to "work out," the blackish discolorations thus caused are very disappointing. With caution, both the transparent red and transparent pink can be successfully fired on the gilding metal, sometimes called Tombac The larger the percentage of alloy, which may be tin or antimony as well as zinc, the lighter and brighter the transparent red, but unfortunately the risk of cracking and breaking away is also increased

PURPLE

Opaque purples and lavenders are not common in enamels. They are compounded from the oxides of manganese, such as black binoxide of manganese (MnO_2), and usually produce a rather reddish purple. I have never used a brilliant purple opaque enamel and, as far as I know, no company offers such a color. Royal purples and blue purples are seldom seen in older enamels and only occasionally in modern examples Perhaps one should be satisfied with the redder shades of purple and lavender in the opaque enamels now available. There are, however, several very beautiful transparent purples and lavenders These are successful over copper and gold but, strangely enough, many of the transparent purples turn a decided green when applied over fine silver or silver foil.

ENAMELING: *Principles and Practice*

CHARTREUSE

The transparent chartreuse is excellent over silver foil, giving a brilliant effect. Make sure that this color is adequately counter-enameled, as its particular characteristic is to show fine cracks when applied thickly The opaque yellow-greens are soft, but are among the most popular colors for use with the present trend in décor The transparent form of the color over copper is much like flux in appearance and contrasts well with either opaque white or opaque black.

YELLOW

Medium, light, corn and canary yellows are some of the much used shades of yellow opaque enamel. These are apt to be rather hard colors and require longer firing and consequently give trouble in burning out With high firing and additional coats, clear, brilliant yellows in the opaque colors may be successfully added to your enamel palette.

The transparent yellows such as gold yellow and light yellow are not as readily available as they were before World War II. Sodium uranate (Na_2UO_4) is used in some yellows, but, unfortunately, the atom bomb absorbed the supply of uranium. A few good yellows are still available, and for firing directly over copper or over gold foil, there is hardly any color more exciting to the enamelist. On fine silver and, occasionally, on copper the transparent yellows may turn to a dull, muddy finish resembling putty. When this occurs, which is seldom in the first firing, the gloss may sometimes be brought back by an extremely high fire (1600° F. to 1700° F.). If this method does not succeed, it is best to discard the piece or be satisfied with an opaque yellow in place of it.

IVORY

The ivory and cream colors are sold as opaques and are soft, low-fire colors As a background color they are unexcelled. A dark

Characteristics of Certain Enamels

transparent enamel dusted into the ivory background before placing it in the kiln will flatter even the most nondescript design By placing a tray which has an ivory background deep in the kiln and overfiring it, a brilliant transparent color will appear at the edge Turn the tray several times while it is in the kiln and this effective halation can be controlled and continued around the tray Take care not to bring back the opacity of the ivory on the cooler edge near the door of the kiln.

I have included only a few of the more popular colors. There are many more, some which are possibly as satisfactory as those mentioned. Each new color tried will have its peculiarities The above colors have all proved their popularity in the classroom and I would recommend them for the beginner's palette.

VI

MAKING LIMOGES ENAMELS: Preparing the plaque · Counterenameling the plaque · Designing the plaque · Transferring the design · First coat of enamel · Paillons for plaque · Grisaille enameling · Detail painting · Metallic lusters

THE TERM "Limoges enamels" is often used carelessly to describe china painting, miniature portraits and commercially enameled automobile trade-marks True, the term is a broad one, inasmuch as it describes any type of enamel which covers the entire surface, much as we do it today, instead of recessing the colors into pits (champlevé) or separating them by thin wires (cloisonné). As was mentioned in the first chapter, Nardon Penicaud (Penicaud I), ancestor of other famous Penicauds, first used enamel in this way (*Fig* 48) in Limoges, France, at the end of the Fifteenth Century. His method was to fuse a layer of opaque white over the entire surface; then, by using a black oxide or some finely ground enamel, he would draw his outline and also suggest anatomical forms and details. Over this, he would then place his transparent colors and build up the shading, again using opaque white enamels and a covering of thin layers of transparents.

Painting on enamels with finely ground colors was a further development of the Limoges type and followed what we might call the "inlaid" type. The painted enamels usually had a coat of flux as a final protection over the whole piece. Of the works of the Penicauds, as well as many other craftsmen working at that time in France, we have numerous examples in several museums in this country and abroad (*Fig.* 49).

PREPARING THE PLAQUE

In general the execution of a piece of enamel in the Limoges

Making Limoges Enamels

Fig. 48 Triptych—Crucifixion, St. John and St. Catherine, Fifteenth Century. An early example of Limoges painted enamel (*Courtesy The Taft Museum, Cincinnati*)

tradition is done in the way described in the following paragraphs. The plaque or panel to be used is first cleaned in the manner outlined in Chapter III. However, this time added care is taken to remove the tarnished areas near the edge. When planning a panel which will eventually be set in a bezel, or ring of metal, it is advisable to turn the edges over with a sloping but not too abrupt curve, using the small rounded end of a chasing hammer (*Fig. 50*). The thickness of the copper has much to do with the method of forming the turned-down edge. For panels up to one square inch the thinner gauge is adequate and insures a neater job so I would suggest using at least 22-gauge copper. It is surprising how thin the copper can be and still form a stable, solid plaque. Even though enamel is known to be very elastic the combination of the counterenamel and the surface enamel together tend to give

ENAMELING: *Principles and Practice*

Fig. 49 Ewer—Nude Men in Combat, PIERRE REYMOND, Sixteenth Century, French Limoges A unique example of enameling on a complicated basic form. (*Courtesy The Taft Museum, Cincinnati*)

enough strength for our purpose. As the size of panel is increased, a heavier gauge will add greater strength and help to avoid warping. Panels up to 30 or 40 square inches are perfectly safe on 18-gauge copper, for larger panels one might use 16 gauge.

Flat panels of the Limoges type may be done successfully on discarded etching plates. During the period of World War II, when copper was at a premium, many of us in the enameling field received from museums old copper etching plates ranging up to 14-gauge. They made perfect enameling plates and, being heavy needed no turning at the edges. However, the turned edge (*Fig. 51*) has four valuable uses: 1. it keeps the plate from warping and strengthens the outer edge, 2. it enables the bezel to turn against a neat, even surface as the enamel tends to flow down over the curve, 3. there is more richness and depth to the piece which is formed in this way than when it is left flat and 4. it greatly

Making Limoges Enamels

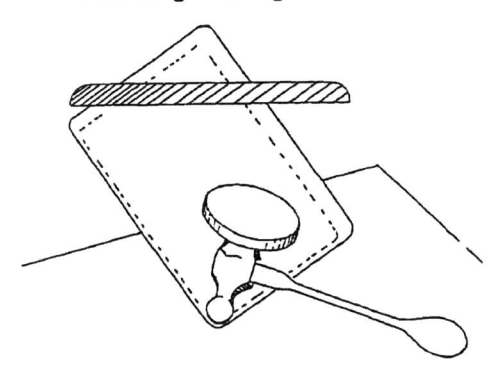

Fig. 50 The chasing hammer is used for turning down edges and rounding corners of the Limoges panel

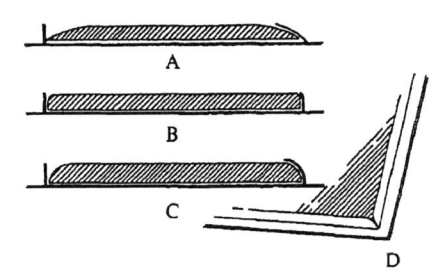

Fig. 51 A. Edge of enamel plaque not sufficiently turned down B. Edge too abrupt C Appropriate shaping for good bezel fitting D. File a V shape from corners of the bezel

facilitates firing and prevents the plaque from adhering to any platform or mica used in the kiln.

For more serious and thorough workmanship, these panels of copper and, more especially, gold are not hammered down at their edges but bent up and soldered at their corners (*Fig.* 52) To do this, measure carefully ⅛ inch or less from each side for the edge to be turned down and score deeply on the line with any sharp-edged tool. Cut out the square remaining in the corners and with a fine jeweler's triangular file, bevel these edges to form a 45° angle. When folded up as a box the sides will fit exactly. Flow hard solder (flow point 1460° F.) along the fold and into

ENAMELING: *Principles and Practice*

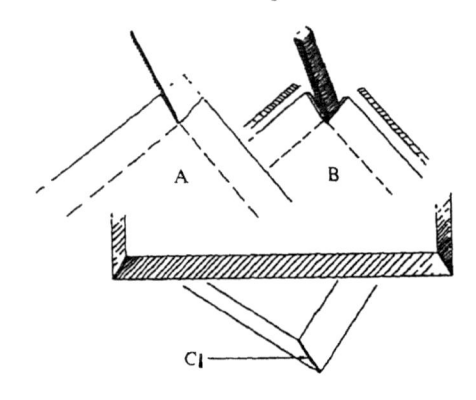

Fig 52 A Saw slightly less than square from the corners B. Bevel edges with a file C Solder corners with the hardest solder.

the corners, and your plate is formed securely. It will never lose shape nor show any unevenness in the many firings it may receive. If the piece is round, as in the case of a brooch or circular picture, the forming and selection of gauge is much the same. Dome slightly in the center and curve more abruptly near the circumference (*Fig.* 53).

I have dwelt at some length on shaping the plaque because I feel that even before starting to enamel one should visualize some three-dimensional richness or exaggeration. Work done on a flat piece of metal and mounted in a low bezel sacrifices much beauty

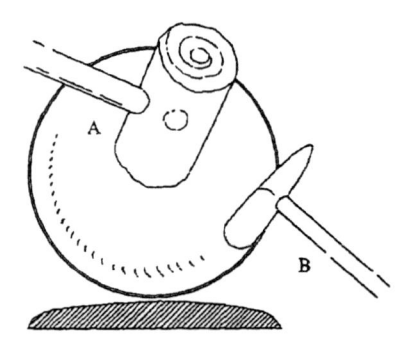

Fig. 53 Shaping Circular Form for Limoges Plaque A. Use large rawhide mallet in the center B. Use smaller wooden mallet at the edge.

96

Making Limoges Enamels

of depth in the color. It might as well be a scratched design on a piece of cardboard. When setting plaques, brooches or small panels, the pieces should be raised forward as much as possible to intensify the illusion of depth which enamel gives to color so beautifully Here is the place to dramatize this rare quality rather than minimize it. Stoning with Carborundum, described in Chapter VII on cloisonné enameling, produces a perfect domelike surface and enhances the depth of color.

COUNTERENAMELING THE PLAQUE

To go on with the Limoges process, we must now apply the counterenamel In washing the colors the milky substance which separates from the rest of the enamel has to be completely eliminated This is actually composed of very fine particles of enamel and perhaps bits of soda and potash which have been disengaged in the commercial grinding. During the hand-grinding process the milky substance is continually being washed away. Enamels should be thoroughly washed each time they are used. To wash colors, place the enamel in a small jar and flush vigorously with water, at the same time stirring with the spatula. Let this settle for about ten seconds and pour away any milky liquid. Continue this process until the water looks clear The muddy residue taken from the enamels can be used for counterenamel, but one point must be made quite clear—the amount, hardness and evenness of the counterenamel should be as nearly like the enamel which is anticipated for the front as possible (*Fig. 54*). I am giving a rule here which is so often overlooked by students in my classes The severe tensions to which the metal as well as the glazes will be subjected, along with the sudden shocks it receives by constantly being taken in and out of the kiln, make it imperative that the chances for failure from these causes be minimized as much as possible. I suggest that if the sludge, or washings from the enamels, is utilized as counterenamel, a thin coat of flux of a coarser mesh be used also. Fire the counterenamel only to the fusing point. This creates less fire glaze on the face of your panel, which may then be cleaned more easily.

ENAMELING *Principles and Practice*

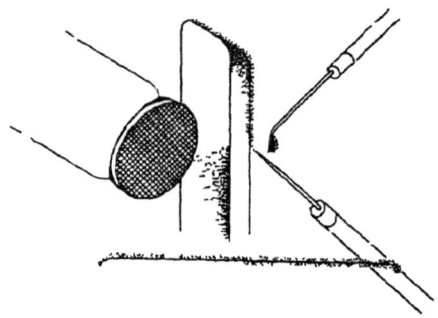

Fig. 54 Counterenamel (by dusting) and front enamel (by spatula and pointer) should be equivalent in depth, hardness, and amount

DESIGNING THE PLAQUE

After we have finished the counterenamel and have cleaned the top surface we are now ready to proceed with the Limoges composition As with any design to be applied, a complete painting in color is rendered on paper first. Not only is the design colored with regard to what can be produced in enamel, but each color is matched to the exact hue and value of the enamel test you have before you. The completed rendering in tempera or water color is your master working drawing. I would not make the statement that variations, accidents and deviation from this working drawing should never be allowed and no artist would care to be so dogmatic. However, it is during the creation of the composition that emotional expression should be encouraged rather than while actually applying the enamel. It is difficult to correct weaknesses in a hastily rendered design during the enameling process.

TRANSFERRING THE DESIGN

The problem at present is of transferring the design from the working drawing to the copper plate. If it is an elaborate composition involving much subtlety of line and shape, use the following method Transfer your composition to tracing paper. Place a sheet of carbon paper between the tracing and the copper plate and trace over the design with a blunt steel stylus With a jeweler's scriber or your enameling pointer next retrace your carbon line

98

Making Limoges Enamels

on the copper, leaving a visible engraved line. Be sure to remove all remains of carbon before enameling by repeating the cleaning process as formerly described. As stated before, carbon in any form is disastrous to enamel, leaving a row of tiny bubbles wherever it is present.

One may also draw by freehand with a lithograph pencil or a china marking pencil, like those used in stores for pricing glass merchandise, and then make the engraved line with the scriber. Grease from such a pencil line can be removed with household ammonia before cleaning the copper in the usual manner. The line so engraved will show clearly through a thin coat of flux or any light transparent enamel. The Limoges enamel may also start with an entire coat of opaque white or opaque black Transferring the design onto this surface becomes more difficult. One method is to use red carbon paper which is obtainable in most stationery stores. A thin black line is sometimes drawn with overglaze paint, liquid platinum or metallic gold or, if necessary, certain focal points may be placed with the dividers, locating the position of the paillons by actual measurement This gives sufficient key lines and points to enable one to fill in the remainder of the design freehand.

FIRST COAT OF ENAMEL

With the motifs or figures plotted we lay in the first coat of colors. Working over an enameled surface instead of laying your first coat directly on the copper is one way to save much time and distress and to avoid bubbles forming where the colors join. One coat of colors when fired over the flux should come from the kiln clean and bright, by contrast with the rather disappointing result when done directly on copper. This is because so many of the soft, or low-fire, colors burn away before the harder colors become fused Do not be too discouraged. The numerous firings to come will improve the appearance of your panel.

Very thin layers of enamel are added each time, particularly the transparents. Several thick layers of color will destroy the glassy depth and become semiopaque.

Each time any one of the colors is re-enameled, the remaining

ENAMELING: *Principles and Practice*

colors are also re-enameled. The entire surface is thus brought to the same level, following the true Limoges technique. Enameled panels having several different levels are sometimes interesting and novel but they are a departure from the method under discussion.

We have now brought all of the basic colors to a point where we wish to leave them for a final effect. It may have taken five or even more firings. The various textures have been obtained by allowing undercoats to show through, some areas to remain with burned patches, softer colors to bleed into harder colors, or many other interesting accidents. In regard to the burned patches, these are especially effective in opaque red, which is sometimes richer as a partially burned color than as a clear solid red.

PAILLONS FOR PLAQUE

We proceed with the next step which is to apply the paillons of silver or gold foil. By your tests you have learned that transparent cold colors are most satisfactory over silver foil and ruby red, purples and gold yellows over the gold foil. Plan your composition accordingly.

Now that our paillons must take on more elaborate shapes, some mention should be made of the process already described in some detail in Chapter IV. Trace on thin tracing paper or onionskin from your detailed working drawing the exact shape needed for the paillon. Cut with curved manicure scissors or a razor blade, always holding the foil between two pieces of tracing paper since it is too thin to manage otherwise. Here the importance of the original design is demonstrated inasmuch as it was there that these pailloned areas were planned. The simpler the shapes are devised in the first place, the easier they will be to cut out (*Fig. 55*). The foil can be overlapped but, even so, try to plan manageable shapes for cutting. Fine lines and particularly tortuous, twisted lines do not lend themselves well to paillons and should be rendered in some other manner.

If there are any bubbles or pits in the enamel over which the paillons are to be fired, they should be eliminated by first patching and then refiring. In applying the paillons to the basic colors,

Making Limoges Enamels

care should be taken to remove all air pockets before firing. This is done by dabbing the foil, after it is in place, with absorbent cotton or a soft rag. The effect of air pockets being formed under the foil as the paillons adhere is similar to miniature mountains or volcanos which increase in size after each firing Care should be taken never to let the temperature exceed 1400° F. when the paillons are exposed as the metal foils burn very easily. Bring your panel out of the kiln several times for the burnishing process By this simple method of burnishing, or smoothing down, with the dull kitchen knife until the foil is evenly laid, you will be rewarded with as smooth a surface as is possible to attain with foil. Do not try to fire silver or gold foil over some of the very soft colors such as opaque red or soft opaque white, because the foil will burn as the soft colors mature. It is better to use flux or any hard transparent color

Fig 55 Keep silver paillons (represented by shaded areas) in any composition very simple in shape.

GRISAILLE ENAMELING

At this stage, the true Limoges enamelers adopted a method called grisaille. It was simply the process of building up a shaded quality to the areas of color by adding opaque white, sometimes thickly and sometimes thinly enough for the color beneath to

ENAMELING: *Principles and Practice*

show through. The opaque white for this purpose must be a dense white or one which will fuse to a shiny surface but not become absorbed by the coating of enamel upon which it is placed. The opaque white for shading must be extremely fine, almost like face powder With an agate mortar and pestle, first grind the enamel as fine as you can and then reduce to an impalpable fineness by grinding on a glass slab with a flexible spatula.

DETAIL PAINTING

It is possible to buy the enamels already ground to powder fineness or in paste form. These fine enamels if suspended in an oil are ready for use or, if dry, can be mixed with a drop of squeegee oil as a binder and oil of lavender as an extender and applied as an overglaze for all of the refinements. shadings, anatomical detail and features. Care is needed in firing these delicate colors whether the opaque white underpainting is used, as in the original Limoges enamels, or eliminated, as in most modern interpretations The finely ground colors applied at this stage can either "make or break" your entire piece. Overpainting left only partially fired leaves a rough finish, which is unsatisfactory. Deep cracks may be avoided by bringing the panel to a rather sudden heat immediately upon putting it into the kiln. In this way, the cracks which do occur are eliminated by the immediate flowing together of the enamel Avoid placing the panel in a cold kiln and bringing up the heat gradually, for the original cracks may remain open long enough for the copper to oxidize, leaving most distressing black crevices.

After the overpainting colors have fused into the under enamels and their cracks in turn have flowed together, withdraw the piece from the kiln immediately. Do not linger or the delicate surface colors will flow, distorting the original shape and ruining your fine detail. These colors also have a tendency to sink down into the basic enamels if overfired, leaving a depression on the surface of your panel wherever they were placed.

METALLIC LUSTERS

The finishing touches are fired with metallic paints, sometimes

Making Limoges Enamels

called metallic lusters (*Fig.* 56) These are available in several colors, the most commonly used being gold. The platinum gives a dark steel-gray line and some of the copper lusters are very effective, being warmer shades than the gold. The lusters were originally made by grinding up gold leaf with honey on a glass slab and later washing the honey away. The gold was then mixed with oxgall, sugar candy, gum arabic, glycerine, water and a few drops of oil of lavender. The lusters used today are essentially the same composition and can be applied with a brush or pen. For this purpose I use a No. 00 sable brush from which I have pulled out all but about twelve hairs. The pen used depends upon the type of line desired.

Always apply the lusters to the enamel in the *thinnest possible* coat. As the gold particles are bound to settle to the bottom of the vial, a vigorous shaking or stirring of the luster before using is recommended Using only the vehicle, when little or no gold is

Fig. 56 Staff of Life, KENNETH F. BATES, 1950. Metallic luster applied with a fine pen was used throughout this panel.

stirred into it, will cause the gold to disappear in the firing. The largest per cent of failure is caused by an incomplete *drying* of the gold If no special timing has been determined by experimentation, it is far safer to allow the gold to dry overnight or even longer. One may also dry the gold at a temperature of approximately 300° F. or less for one hour. Commercially, the metallic colors are dried for a much longer period.

The metallic lusters are properly developed at 1140° F. for five minutes, but so much depends on the hardness or softness of the enamel upon which the luster is placed that I find there is really no hard and fast rule. On most transparent enamels the above firing table is safe. Often work is ruined by the improper firing of the gold luster.

As the enamel will crack when the gold lines are fired, one must necessarily raise the heat until the cracks thus formed in the enamel disappear Subsequent firings will not destroy the gold.

For a silver line I use one of the newly created conductive coating materials containing a specially prepared silver powder. This is by no means an enamel, but merely a coating used commercially to produce a surface of low electrical resistance and high conductivity when applied to such base materials as porcelain, glass, plastics and metals. These conductive coatings contain enough silver to fire to a dull white at about 1400° F. After the dull mat finish is produced a final high gloss is achieved by rubbing with an agate burnisher.

I recommend using limited quantities of gold, platinum, copper or silver lusters. Abundant use of the gold luster in particular produces a very cheap effect. One should not resort to outlining with this material to any great extent, as it is a falsification of the cloisonné technique. At best it can never improve a poor design or strengthen a weak composition.

Study of specific examples may further clarify the uses made of the Limoges method. The scalloped plate, *Fruits of My Orchard* (*Fig.* 39B), shows the Limoges technique followed to a certain extent. The colors of each fruit vary, being both transparent and opaque. They were finely ground and applied over a base coat of soft-fire light turquoise, which blended into low-fire

Making Limoges Enamels

white opaque at the edge. All detail and outlines were worked with platinum luster, but no paillons were employed.

Argument in a Limoges Market Place (Fig 57) represents an abstract conception of market women in a heated discussion over the price of cabbages. This subject is the seventh episode musically portrayed in a set of piano pieces called *Pictures from an Exhibition,* composed by Modest Petrovitch Moussorgsky. The Limoges manner of working was chosen because of the association of subject matter The use of an undercoat of opaque white was not employed in this case, instead, each color was inlaid directly on the copper. It is possible to detect from the reproduction (notably a costume directly below the Tabac sign) areas which were allowed to burn at their edges, giving a sort of halation. The solid enamel undercoat method sacrifices this opportunity for nuances of color, texture, and burned areas obtained with opaque red and other soft opaques.

Fig. 57 Argument in a Limoges Market Place, KENNETH F. BATES, 1944. A panel developed in the Limoges manner showing colors juxtaposed. (*Courtesy Cleveland Museum of Art*)

ENAMELING: *Principles and Practice*

In *Inception of Spring* (Fig. 58) a complete Limoges handling was carried out, beginning with a base of opaque white and working up with gradual steps through the transparents, opaques, paillons, overpainting, and metallics. This small piece measuring 3" x 5½" involved eighteen firings and more than sixty hours of work. It depicts the revival of the forces of Nature in spring with its fecundity and turbulence. Inasmuch as many fine lines and details were needed to properly portray such a subject, the original Limoges technique was chosen

Fig. 58 Inception of Spring, KENNETH F. BATES, 1946. The panel, which is 3 inches by 5½ inches, describes the fecundity and turbulence of Spring. Here the original technique of Limoges enameling was followed conscientiously

Making Limoges Enamels

The famous Limousin portraits of the Limoges school done in the late Fifteenth Century and early Sixteenth Century were extraordinary examples of skill and control of the medium. *Portrait of a Lady* (*Fig.* 59) is one example of this period. In a more abstract contemporary manner the Limoges portrait technique was adapted to the study of three Siamese cats watching a bird outside the window (*Fig.* 60).

Fig. 59 *Portrait of a Lady,* LEONARD LIMOUSIN, early Sixteenth Century. Léonard Limousin was the most celebrated of the Limoges enamelers and often received royal patronage. (*Courtesy Metropolitan Museum of Art*)

ENAMELING: *Principles and Practice*

The field of portraits in enamel done in the Limoges method could be explored by some ambitious enameler today, as there are comparatively few good modern examples.

Fig. 60 *The Bird Watch,* KENNETH F. BATES, 1949. Stylized portraits of three Siamese cats watching a bird outside the window.

VII

MAKING CLOISONNÉ ENAMELS BY THE OLDER TECHNIQUE AND A MODERN VERSION:
Forming panels · Cleaning the gold · Wire for cloisonné · Soldering cloisonné wires · Applying the enamel · Firing cloisonné · Stoning process · Shorter cloisonné method

FEW INDEED are the crafts which have changed less through the ages than the craft of making cloisonné enamels. The procedure to be described here would undoubtedly be quite familiar to an Eleventh-Century Byzantine artisan working in this medium (*Fig.* 61). Our convenient electric kilns, which operate at the turning of a switch, and the mechanical devices for grinding and manufacturing the frit itself shorten the hours of labor, yet the final results are much the same The actual process of application and firing is unchanged.

Names of all the techniques in enameling are French. Cloisonné is derived from the French *cloisons*, meaning "partitioned areas" with reference to the fact that each color is enclosed in a space, or cell. The word today connotes a handmade process but one often hears it applied to all sorts of manufactured colored jewelry. Even transparent plastics set over painted designs for compacts, etc. are miscalled cloisonné by some.

The most superb examples of cloisonné, namely the Byzantine, were made on pure gold. This is the metal recommended although fine silver works equally well. Copper, too, may be used but it seems hardly fine enough to warrant the painstaking process. Copper and sterling silver have the common disadvantage of oxidizing when brought to maximum heat. It then becomes quite difficult to polish the many exposed wire surfaces.

Here a word should be said about the character of a cloisonné design (*Fig.* 62). A certain flowing quality must be realized.

ENAMELING: *Principles and Practice*

Fig 61 A gold cloisonné enameled medallion which was originally part of the border of an Icon, Byzantine, late Eleventh Century. (*Courtesy Metropolitan Museum of Art*)

A   B

Fig 62 Cloisonné Designs   A. Inappropriate design for cloisonné enamel technique   B. Motif suitable for cloisonné.

Sacrifices and compromises are made to accommodate the design to the use of bent or curved lines, rather than of angular or broken lines. Avoid sharp turns and do not worry about anatom-

Making Cloisonné Enamels

ical detail, but let the movements and rhythms be created by the wire

FORMING PANELS

As in the case of the Limoges enamels described in the last chapter, let us begin by forming a small panel upon which we intend to build the cloisonné design. The panel should be 20 gauge, or .032 inches thick. Either form the panel as previously described, by scoring and folding the edges down, or keep the base flat and solder a strip around the outside of the panel, forming a kind of fence. The latter method is used when the panel is not to be set in a bezel, such as an earring drop or a brooch (*Fig.* 63) The first method is preferred (i.e., preparing the plate exactly as

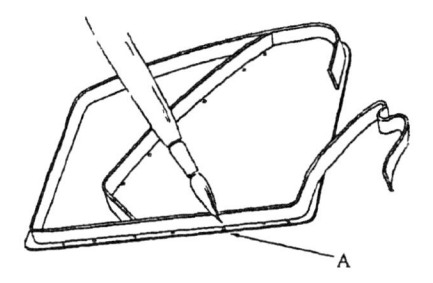

Fig 63 Solder a strip of metal around the edge of the cloisonné plaque A. Keep solder away from enamel wherever possible.

for a Limoges panel), leaving the surface fairly rough, especially in gold work. Too smooth and polished a surface before enameling invites chipping and a poor adhesion to the metal.

The use of the 24-carat gold, or fine gold, has a definite purpose Regardless of the number of times it is heated it never blackens, or oxidizes, in the process. Carat in gold signifies the amount by weight of gold, as distinguished from the alloy (either silver or copper) which has been added. In other words, 12-carat gold signifies that one half the weight is gold. By keeping in mind that any pure metal melts at a higher temperature than an alloy, one may avoid many difficulties in enameling and soldering.

ENAMELING. *Principles and Practice*

It is always a delight to work with fine gold for enameling. No cleaning or filing of edges is required between firings and there is no danger of marring your enamel with specks of fire glaze as in the case of copper work. Such ease of procedure does not, however, release the craftsman from his constant attention to immaculate cleanliness. Unkempt workbenches, soiled hands, and dull tools are not the mark of a good craftsman whose job requires meticulous attention to detail.

CLEANING THE GOLD

Gold is cleaned by a slow, steady pickling in a dilute nitric acid solution of one part acid to ten parts water. The pickle is kept over a low flame in a Pyrex container and never brought to the boiling point. Keep the solution available for the many cleanings needed later. Let the gold remain in the solution until the panel becomes a light-yellow color. For a rougher surface, scratch with coarse steel wool or a glass brush. This often brings out a more pleasing quality to the transparent colors than a highly glossed surface

WIRE FOR CLOISONNÉ

The wire used to enclose each color in the design is soldered onto the panel before the enamel is applied. First a rough estimate must be taken to judge the length of wire needed. This is easily accomplished with a string roughly covering each outline in your working drawing. When straightened the string gives some idea of the amount of wire required. The length of the outline may seem surprisingly great and could certainly be underestimated unless some such trial measurement is made. This wire must also be of fine gold. Although it is very soft its strength is sufficient after being imbedded in the enamel. Carefully consider both the height and thickness of the wire. I recommend that the wire be 30-gauge wide and 18-gauge high, or .010 inch by .040 inch. To be extravagant in the height of the fine gold wire is absurd, inasmuch as it will be filed away and can not be resold for

Making Cloisonné Enamels

scrap gold The high cost of gold makes it good practice to use a bench apron for catching all scraps and filings.

Following the master drawing, which is so developed that each outline forms a definite area, bend the ribbonlike wire into shape. I find that the wires can be bent into the exact shapes desired by placing them directly onto the line drawing (preferably drawn in India ink on white paper) and forming them with jeweler's tweezers The wire is readily cut with ordinary manicure scissors. By holding the wire designs on a steel block and tapping slightly with the flat end of a chasing hammer, you can quickly level them into one horizontal plane.

SOLDERING CLOISONNÉ WIRES

Each wire shape is now placed on the plate and soldered in its proper location It is well to tip the joinings of the wires with hard solder to make sure that they do not change their position after the enamel has fused. As 24-carat gold does not melt until 1945° F. gold of a lesser carat should be used as a solder. The best results are obtained with a 14-carat, pale yellow-gold solder having a flow point of 1515° F or a 16-carat solder which flows at 1500° F. The temperature required for general enameling purposes will be less than the flowing point of these solders. Borax is still the best flux for all hard soldering but the pure gold cloisons are of such a delicate nature that they require careful workmanship. The heat of the blowtorch must always be applied from below (*Fig.* 64). Heat from above causes the solder to flow onto the wires, leaving the plate free, and risks burning the fine wires before the soldering is completed.

Clean away any remaining borax by immersing again in the nitric-acid pickle, and file around the joints. We are now ready for the enameling.

Counterenamel the gold panel after first roughing the surface. Again, be reminded that the amount and the hardness of the counterenamel should be as nearly similar to that of the surface enamel as possible (*Fig.* 54). A disappointing feature of enameling is the occurrence of cracks, which reveal themselves after the piece is finished and polished.

ENAMELING. *Principles and Practice*

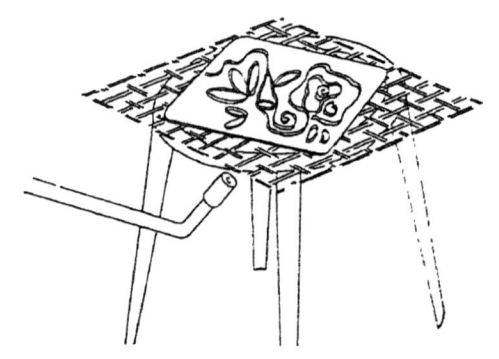

Fig. 64 Solder the cloisonné wires to the base with heat from below.

APPLYING THE ENAMEL

The colors which are to be laid into the cloisons are now ground to a fineness which is commensurable with the scale of your design. The usual 60 mesh would be too coarse for the size of wire already suggested. Place the enamel in a small Wedgwood mortar and cover with water. Grind carefully with the pestle, washing at regular intervals, until about as fine as table salt (*Fig.* 65). Now transfer the enamel to an agate mortar and pestle for finer grinding if necessary. Another way to obtain fine

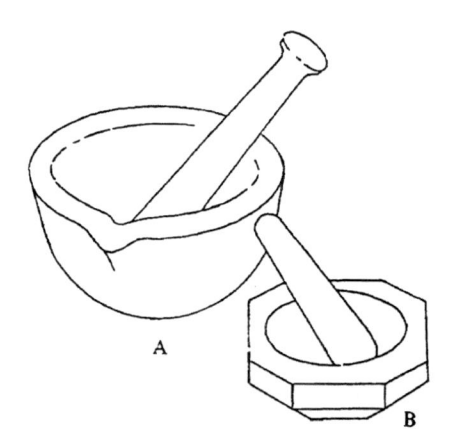

Fig. 65 Grinding the Enamel A. First grind the enamel for cloisonné work in a Wedgwood mortar and pestle with water B. For a final grinding use an agate mortar and pestle.

Making Cloisonné Enamels

enamel is to strain through various mesh silks until the required fineness is reached The enamel thus sifted must be thoroughly washed, as residual materials, mostly borax and soda, are present in the fine dust To guard against any opacity to your transparent colors wash them with flowing water until any trace of milkiness has disappeared. You will be well compensated for these careful washings when the enamel over fine gold eventually comes from the kiln

With your small spreader and sharpened pointer place each color in its respective position between the gold cloisons Force the fine enamel into the tiny spaces, making sure that no air bubbles are left in or beneath it.

FIRING CLOISONNÉ

There should be no difficulty in the firing. The difference between the melting point of fine gold (1945° F.) and the fusing point of most enamels (1500° F), especially after they have been ground finely and applied thinly, leaves you little concern.

When the first firing is completed you will notice that the enamels have shrunk so that they seem to be clinging to the wire cloisons. To build the enamel up to the level of the wire, the plate or panel will need complete re-enameling. Possibly a third coat of enamel will be necessary (*Fig 66*)

As the succeeding coats are built up, it sometimes enriches the color to work in different tones. For rich greens, make the first coats light blue and proceed to deep greens. The warmth of the gold will enrich the greens when developed this way. Some transparent purples are improved by first placing a coat of transparent pink over the gold. Flux will not come as a pure white over gold, because the yellow color of the metal naturally shows through. One coat of opaque white and two coats of flux will, however, approximate the transparent white quality. Take care to use the thinnest possible layers of color when building up with several coats as the tiny areas lose all transparency if applied too thickly. For contrast some areas need to be done in the opaque enamels. The intense brilliancy of transparents over the gold de-

ENAMELING: *Principles and Practice*

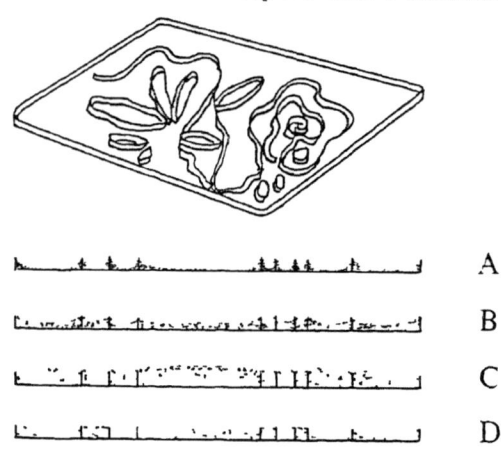

Fig 66 Cloisonné Enameling A Enamel clings to wires in first firing B Enamel fills the cloisons in second or third firing C Enamel heaps up after the fourth firing D The enamel must be stoned down to the level of the wires.

mands such relief The final coating of enamel is now fired and has reached a height where it seems to bulge above the wires. (*Fig. 66c*).

STONING PROCESS

The next procedure is to stone the enamel down to the level of the wires (*Fig. 66D*). With the enamel firmly gripped in one hand and a medium coarse Carborundum stone in the other, place both hands in a deep bowl of water or under running water, and grind with a circular motion (*Fig. 67*). When opaques are used with the transparents be sure that the fine grains of opaque are not ground into the transparents. Running water flushes away all of these finely ground particles and is by far the better method.

You must stone until all wires are evenly exposed and until all mounds and depressions in the surface of the enamels have disappeared Occasional drying will reveal to you how much more stoning there is to be done. As the enamel approaches the level of the gold wires substitute fine Carborundum stone for the medium

116

Making Cloisonné Enamels

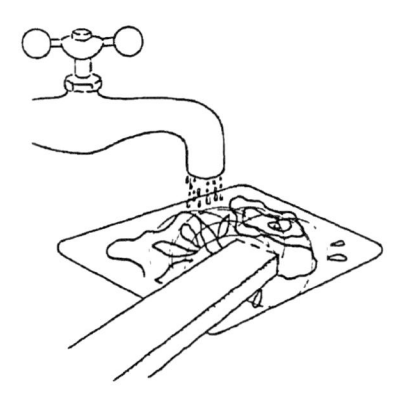

Fig 67 Stone cloisonné enamel under running water with Carborundum, using a circular motion.

stone. The purpose for changing to a finer Carborundum is to avoid the danger of burring the edges of the wire Such a burred edge gives the appearance of thickness to the wire and your work will lose its refinement Fire now before applying more enamel so that scratches left by the stoning will not show under the last enamel coating The stoning will usually reveal some pits and air bubbles These should be refilled before this firing If any overpainting or fine overglazes are contemplated for accents, they should be done at this point.

The old cloisonné enamels, particularly the Chinese (*Fig.* 68), were not refired after the final stoning but polished instead. The use of pumice or rotten stone with water or oil as a medium was rubbed over the surface of the stoned enamel to bring up the finish I prefer to buff the wires with tripoli, using a felt buffer. No damage seems to be done to the enamel by this method

SHORTER CLOISONNÉ METHOD

To modernize the cloisonné process somewhat, there are a few short cuts which could be mentioned. In the first place, I find that it is not necessary to solder all the separate wires end to end nor down onto the base The plate itself in this case is copper, only

ENAMELING: *Principles and Practice*

Fig 68 *The Herd Boy on His Water Buffalo.* An example of Seventeenth-Century Chinese cloisonné enamel. The metal is gilded bronze.

the cloisonné wires being of fine gold. I use a thin coat of medium-soft opaque white for the first layer. After the opaque white is fired it should be stoned to a perfectly flat level surface and refired for patches or bubbles. Now make a mixture of thick gum tragacanth about the consistency of mucilage. Form each wire but do not solder the joints. Place them on your panel, allowing the tragacanth to harden and thus hold them in place for firing.

As the wires in this case are not soldered end to end, your motifs and shapes will have to be revised to meet the conditions of the wire (*Fig.* 69). No straight line, or fence as it were, can

118

Making Cloisonné Enamels

Fig 69 When the wires are not soldered to the base metal for cloisonné enameling, the motif may incorporate loose or broken lines.

stand upright by itself. The wire must bend in at least one place. However, the ends seem to fit closely enough without soldering, which eliminates one step from the older method.

For a still shorter method and, in some cases, a very interesting modern version of cloisonné, leave the wires exposed and apply only one layer of enamel This effect is not true cloisonné but presents a surface treatment worthy of experimentation. After the copper backing has been enameled with opaque white and the cloisonné held in place by the gum tragacanth, the piece is thoroughly dried and fired at about 1200° F. In this process the wires settle and fuse to the enamel. The risk in this method is that the shapes may change position as the enamels are placed between them. To avoid this, fill in all of the enamels at the same time, keeping them level To obtain transparency foil is applied after one or two coats have partially built up the enamel. Then only one thin coat of transparent enamel is given.

The succeeding illustrations (*Figs*. 70-76) serve to describe the method of cloisonné enameling more adequately than words. They picture the making of one of the seven panels for a small gold cloisonné box set on an ebony block (*frontispiece*). This box was designed and executed for the late Mrs. Benjamin P. Bole in appreciation for her patronage of the arts in Cleveland.

ENAMELING: *Principles and Practice*

The author was commissioned by the Cleveland Museum of Art and the Cleveland Institute of Art in much the same way that a Renaissance craftsman was sponsored.

Fig 70 shows the way the spreader and spatula are used to apply the counterenamel. The small panels (1" × 1¾") were formed in the method described—ruled, scored, folded up, and soldered with hard solder. Notice in *Fig.* 70₁ that the copper is rough and still retains the coarse marks of the rasping file. In *Fig.* 70₂ the first coat of counterenamel has been fired. Here the counterenamel was planned as an integral part of the whole design. It was of brilliant opaque vermilion left exposed for the inside of the box and also placed on four projecting cantilevers so that it reflected upon plain areas of polished gold. The reddish flash of the counterenamel on the gold was essential to the color unity of the design. As the opaque vermilion is a soft, or low-fire enamel, it tends to burn out in the first firing (*Fig.* 70₂); consequently, the second coat was applied (*Fig.* 70₃).

In *Fig.* 71 the fine gold wire is bent into shape. The small panel shown with its outline rendering required twelve inches of wire

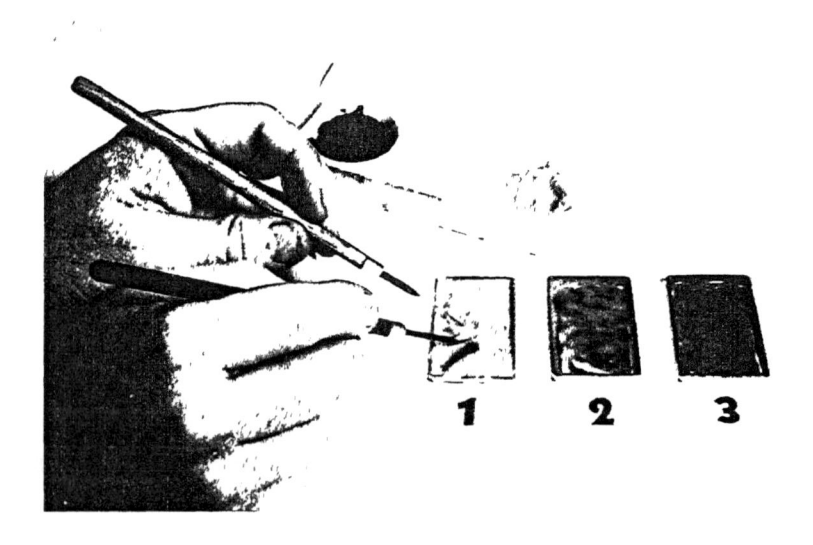

Fig. 70 1. Place the counterenamel on the panels 2. Fire the first coat of counterenamel 3. Fire the second coat.

120

Making Cloisonné Enamels

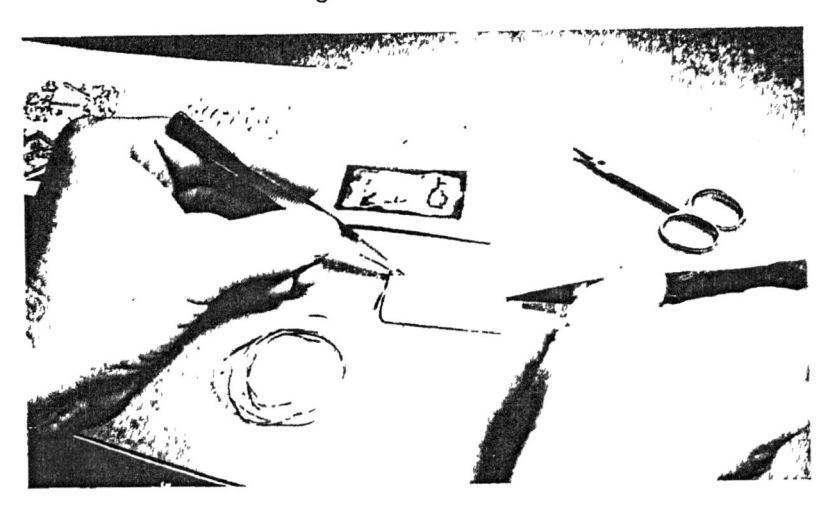

Fig. 71 Bend the cloisonné wire, or ribbon, into shape using tweezers. Follow the original drawing carefully.

Tweezers are the most convenient tools for handling the wire, which, in this case, was .010 inch wide and .040 inch high. Ordinary manicure scissors are best for cutting the soft, fine gold wire.

Fig. 72 shows the mortar and pestle for grinding the enamel (*Fig.* 72_2) and the porcelain palette for holding the enamel colors which are mixed with the gum tragacanth (*Fig.* 72_1). *Fig.* 72_3 reveals the roughed copper surface of the face of the panel and *Fig.* 72_4 is the result after two coats of opaque soft white have been fired. In *Fig.* 72_5 the entire set of wires has been bent into shape, placed down on the enameled surface and attached by gently firing them at about 1200° F.

Fig. 73 demonstrates the process of inserting the extra-fine enamel into the cloisonné cells. This is only the first layer, or coat. As the layers are built up with the opaques, the transparent colors are also put in place. These serve to indicate the position of the metal-foil areas.

Fig. 74 shows the panel with its opaque colors completed and the enamels brought up to $\frac{1}{64}$ inch below the height of the wires.

ENAMELING: *Principles and Practice*

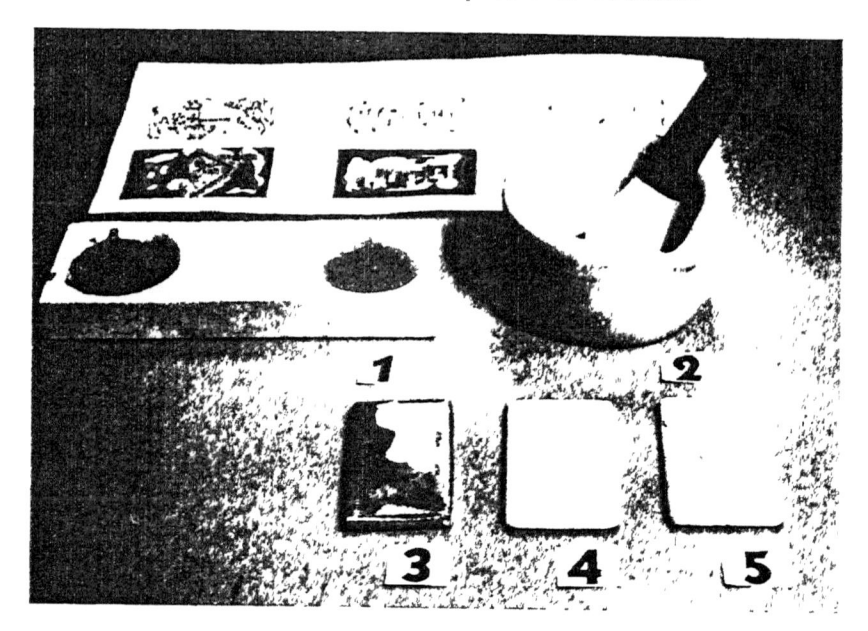

Fig 72 1. Specially ground enamels for cloisonné work   2 Mortar and pestle   3 Leave the surface rough for the first coat of opaque white enamel   4 Panel ready for the wires   5 Gold wires in place.

Fig. 73 Applying the first layer of enamel in the cloisons, or spaces between the wires. The layers of enamel must be built up to meet the level of the wires.

122

Making Cloisonné Enamels

Fig. 74 1 Gold foil 2. Silver foil 3 Foil is cut into tiny squares between thin paper and laid into the areas which will receive the transparent colors 4 A gum tragacanth solution is used to hold the pieces of foil in place.

Now the areas which will be transparent have either gold foil (*Fig.* 74₁) or silver foil (*Fig* 74₂) applied to them Silver foil is always used for cold colors and gold foil for purples, reds and yellows One must cut between tissue paper (*Fig* 74₃) minute bits of foil, as they are to cover completely the small areas where they are required, but not the wires. Some idea of the size of the foil chips may be gained by comparing them with the No. 00 sable brush. After cautiously firing the foils down onto the enamel with tragacanth (*Fig.* 74₁) they are burnished. The transparent enamels, ground exceedingly fine, are applied in a very thin layer, bringing the whole to a level surface In these panels after stoning, I developed detail and shading with overpainting, using fine enamels ground on a glass slab with oil of sassafras for an extender and squeegee oil for a binder. Wires were then buffed as described above and the panels set in the gold box.

ENAMELING: *Principles and Practice*

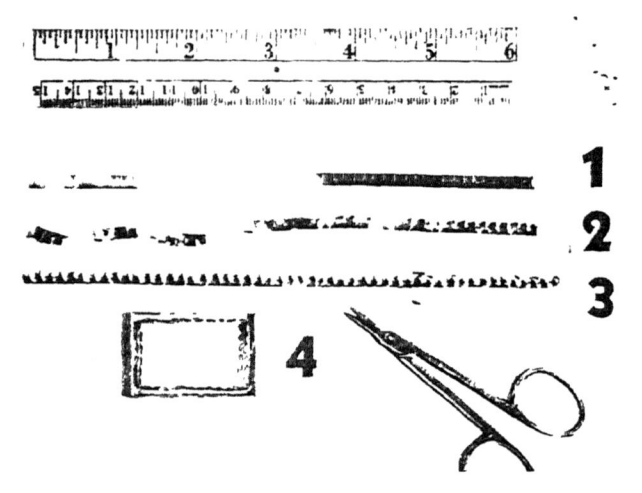

Fig. 75 1. 24-carat gold bezel is first measured   2. Bezel is then cut   3. Each scallop is domed   4. Bezel is soldered into a boxlike shape to receive the enameled plaque.

Narrow ribbons of fine gold, about ⅛ inch wide were used for the bezels (*Fig.* 75). These were marked off at intervals (*Fig.* 75₁), cut into tiny scallops (*Fig.* 75₂), and formed into domes (*Fig.* 75₃). Each domed scallop gave the opportunity for another highlight of gold, which enhanced the sparkle and brilliancy of the enamel. The bezels were soldered into boxlike shapes of gold (*Fig.* 75₄) and, in turn, the enamel was set into the bezels in the same way that one would set a jewel (*Fig.* 76).

Fig. 76 Detail of the finished box showing how the cloisonné enameled panel is set in place

VIII

MAKING CHAMPLEVÉ, *PLIQUE-À-JOUR*, *BASSE-TAILLE* AND OTHER TYPES OF ENAMELS: Design for champlevé · Plating · Preparing the copper · Etching with acid · Enamels for champlevé · Buffing and polishing · *Plique-à-jour* process · *Plique-à-jour* on copper plate · *Plique-à-jour* on mica · *Plique-à-jour* by capillary attraction · Applying the enamel · *Basse-taille* process · Grisaille process · *En résille* process

THE KNIFE, the gouge, the hammer and chisel were the characteristic tools of the Gothic times while the paintbrush was more representative of the Italian Renaissance period. It seems most natural, therefore, that the same sequence in development should be echoed in the field of enameling. In the earlier barbaric and Merovingian enamels a process called champlevé was used, but it was not until the great period of Gothic carved statues and cathedral embellishments that the true art of champlevé flourished (*Fig. 77*). The method was to gouge out with chisels and similar tools recessed areas or cavities from bronze and to fill the hollows with enamel. Gothic craftsmen never recessed the surface deeper than $\frac{1}{20}$ inch. They made more use of opaque colors than transparent ones as the alloyed metal would have caused their clear colors to appear muddy. The remaining Gothic examples are often elaborated with heads and hands cast from the metal and attached to the champlevé enamels with small pegs.

This method of enameling, executed by the hand craftsman, is not commonly seen today although it is used extensively by manufacturers in making a variety of articles ranging from small rings to automobile insignia.

ENAMELING: *Principles and Practice*

Fig 77 Eucharistic Dove, French, Limoges, Thirteenth Century. Champlevé enamel is clearly shown on this copper-gilt piece. In the Middle Ages the consecrated Host was sometimes reserved in a ciborium in the form of a dove, symbol of the Holy Ghost, which was suspended by chains above the altar. By means of a pulley, the dove could be made to descend and ascend. When not in use, it was protected from dust by a small canopy, or curtain, forming a kind of tabernacle. This dove has movable wings. (*Courtesy Metropolitan Museum of Art*)

DESIGN FOR CHAMPLEVÉ

In making the champlevé I suggest that first a design be planned appropriate in character (*Fig. 78*). For this type of enameling it would necessarily be like a stenciled design in that no areas can be overlapped. Remember that this way of using colored enamels shows both exposed metal and shining enamel in constant juxtaposition. One is played against the other. The colors related to the metal areas, particularly the strong opaques, either warm or cold, are bound to be effective. Opaque black or opaque white with primary hues combined with polished copper give the imaginative artist wide scope. Without damage to the

Champlevé, Plique-à-jour, Basse-taille and Other Types

enamels, the exposed copper can be oxidized with liver of sulfur in order to darken it.

PLATING

The exposed areas of metal which are left in the champlevé type of enameling may be plated with silver or gold. Tests have proven that the plating process does not affect most of the enamels. Some of the softer opaques, or low-firing enamels, may become slightly discolored, but, generally speaking, it is safe to say that enamels may be subjected to the plating bath without damage For further precaution a thin coating of paraffin can be applied to the exposed enamel. Remember that any metal which is to be plated must be thoroughly cleaned and polished previous to the plating process Fine silver and gold are equally tempting to the creative designer as he comes to realize the endless possibilities of champlevé enameling

Fig 78 Type of design appropriate for champlevé enameling, showing areas of metal balanced by areas of enamel.

PREPARING THE COPPER

Use copper as a base to work out an example of champlevé enamel First choose a fairly heavy-gauge metal. If it is a small tray which you are making, I suggest at least 18 gauge, for a large tray I suggest 16 gauge. The design motif is transferred

ENAMELING: *Principles and Practice*

with carbon paper onto the copper and then the outline is rescratched with a jeweler's scribe. Or, if you prefer, draw directly with the pencil and scratch the outline over the pencil line. Remove all traces of carbon by the acid bath and regular cleaning processes already described and you are ready to recess the areas for receiving the enamel.

Since acid is used to form the depressions, those parts of the copper that are not to be recessed must be protected. Protective substances for this purpose are called resists A widely used resist is black asphalt paint, which is readily available in paint stores. Paint the asphalt on the areas where the metal is to be retained, being careful to cover all edges and the back of the tray. After letting it dry for a few minutes check the surface to see that no air bubbles remain. These, of course, must be filled.

ETCHING WITH ACID

The exposed copper may be eaten away with a nitric-acid solution of about one part pure nitric acid to three parts water. Weaker solutions give better results than stronger ones for the reason that strong acid disintegrates the copper too rapidly, leaving ragged edges. Immerse the tray in enough acid to cover it. Keep the acid continually moving over the exposed copper with a swab or feather to disperse the tiny air bubbles which form (*Fig.* 79).

Fig 79 As acid eats away the copper, disperse bubbles which form on the surface with a swab.

Champlevé, Plique-à-jour, Basse-taille and Other Types

If bad edges to the pattern result, a carving tool may have to be used to smooth them I am not averse to wavy edges so long as the design is bold enough to accept such freedom

For a more accurate edge, one which will be almost perfect, use ferric chloride in place of the nitric acid This can be purchased from chemical companies and has the appearance of a deep orange-colored salt. Make a saturated solution of equal parts water and ferric chloride, dissolving it in a container large enough to immerse the copper plate.

Unlike the nitric acid etching, this process is slow and your tray may need to be left in the solution for several hours. The side which is to be etched, or eaten away, should be placed downward in the solution so that as the copper disintegrates small particles of it fall away from the tray, leaving a fresh surface for the ferric chloride to eat more deeply.

Allow the acid or other etching mediums to eat down into the copper $\frac{1}{50}$ inch or approximately half the thickness of the metal By occasionally feeling the surface with the fingers during the process, it is not difficult to judge this distance. Wash away the acid with water and proceed to remove the asphalt paint.

A convenient way to remove this paint is to play the blowtorch on it until it carbonizes and then rinse in cold water. Once more the copper is cleaned as before and now we may proceed to apply the enamels.

ENAMELS FOR CHAMPLEVÉ

Use enamels which mature at the same temperature if possible. Lay them carefully and evenly in your recessed areas, bringing them to the level of the copper. For best results each enamel should be ground especially fine so that they will fuse more quickly and evenly. Eighty mesh is too coarse for this purpose. Either the soft or medium-soft enamels work best for the process of champlevé.

From this point on any variety of detail, such as overpainting or luster work, may be applied. The use of foil is also possible (if depth of etching permits), but it must be added after the primary

ENAMELING: *Principles and Practice*

coats and before the last layer of enamel so that in the final result both copper and enamel are brought to the same level.

BUFFING AND POLISHING

Buffing will not pose a problem if one does not overfire the enamels (1600° F. to 1800° F.). Excessive temperatures will cause a tough deposit of fire glaze to form on the exposed copper areas, making it practically impossible to remove without strong acid Some enamels are unharmed by a strong acid bath, but it is extremely hazardous in the case of soft opaques.

For the convex or flat surface, more professional quality is gained by stoning with a Carborundum stone after the last firing. This is an assurance that both the enamel and the exposed metal will be at the same level (*Fig* 80). Follow the stoning process with the usual refire and then polish Buff with the felt wheel, using a good grade of tripoli. Any of the more abrasive buffing compounds are not advisable. They have a tendency to scratch the enamel as the metal areas are being polished.

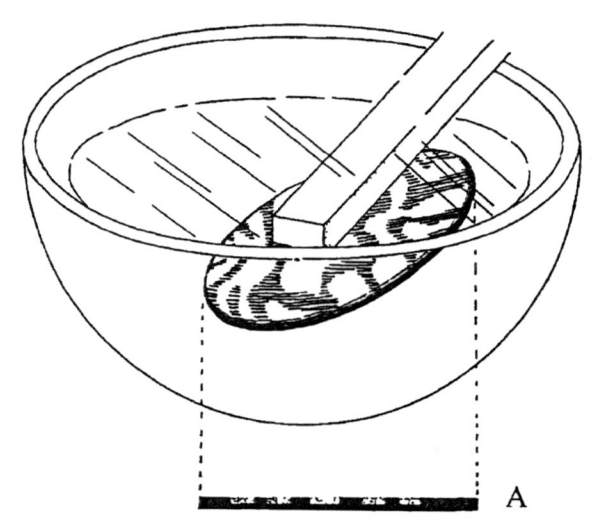

Fig. 80 The champlevé plaque is stoned under water with Carborundum A. Stone until the metal and the enamel are both at the same level.

Champlevé, Plique-à-jour, Basse-taille and Other Types

PLIQUE-À-JOUR PROCESS

Plique-à-jour is the name given to a technique of enameling done in open filigrees which are filled with transparent colors and fired. The effect is that of tiny stained-glass windows. Before trying the *plique-à-jour* style, one should consider its function. The object contemplated must be so viewed or worn that light penetrates it from either side

In the time of the great Italian craftsman, Benvenuto Cellini (1500-1572), skilled artisans often made pieces of jewelry, such as chains, necklaces and earrings, using enameled filigree work to enhance their appearance when held to the light Links in chains or panels set into decorative light fixtures are two suggestions for its use today. Another, and probably the most delightful, use of *plique-à-jour* enameling is the demitasse spoon. The Russian examples of these jewel-like, brilliantly colored spoons are among the most cherished possessions of collectors and museums I have utilized the backless enamel in a small vigil light (*Fig* 81) for the National Naval Medical Center at

Fig. 81 *Vigil Light*, KENNETH F. BATES, 1944. This is backless, or *plique-à-jour*, enameling on fine silver, which shows the perpetually burning light through the tiny openings filled with transparent enamel

ENAMELING· *Principles and Practice*

Bethesda, Maryland. This was fashioned in fine silver and the tiny openings were filled with transparent enamels in cobalt, sapphire, yellow and flux. As a light burns perpetually in this vigil light it was well suited to *plique-à-jour*. The colors of the enamels are always visible in the subdued light of the chapel.

PLIQUE-À-JOUR ON COPPER PLATE

There are several ways in which *plique-à-jour* can be done. One is to build up the filigree, soldering it onto a plate of thin metal (*Fig.* 82). The enamels are next fired in place and then, by covering up the enamel and filigree work with asphalt paint, the back plate is eaten away by acid.

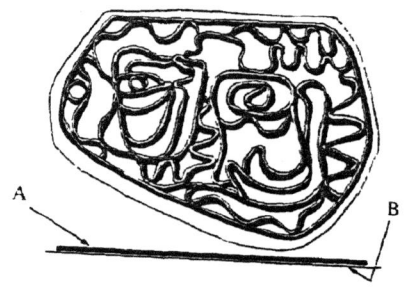

Fig. 82 Design for *Plique-à-jour* Enameling to be Made on a Thin Copper Plate. A. Cover the enamel and the exposed wires with asphalt paint. B. Eat away the thin copper plate with acid, leaving only the enamel held together by the wires and having no backing.

PLIQUE-À-JOUR ON MICA

In the second method the wire filigree is soldered together and placed on a sheet of mica (*Fig.* 83). This holds the grains of enamel in place while firing and can afterwards be removed. Suspend the work on an improvised stand, platform or prongs and give it just enough heat to fuse the enamel. Further heat will make each suspended area of enamel drip. Your only solution then will be to fire it in an inverted position. In case the mica becomes fused to the enamel by high firing the back of the piece must be stoned and placed again in the kiln for its final firing.

Champlevé, Plique-à-jour, Basse-taille and Other Types

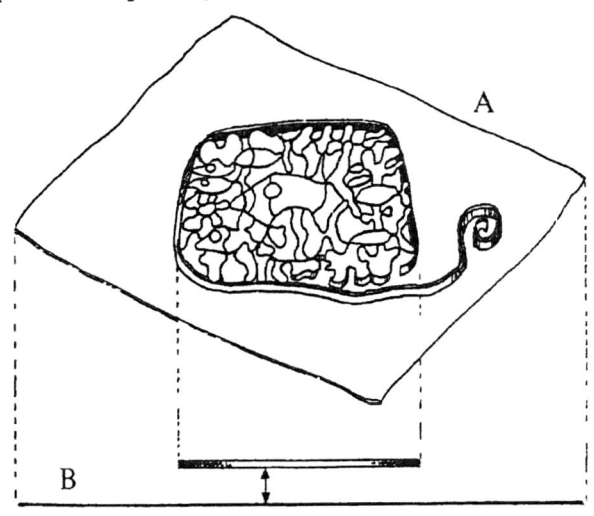

Fig. 83 Method of Firing *Plique-à-jour* Enameling on a Sheet of Mica   A Place the bent wires on a sheet of mica   B. Remove the mica from the enamel after firing.

PLIQUE-À-JOUR BY CAPILLARY ATTRACTION

The third method is that of controlling the size of the openings so that the enamel stays in place by capillary attraction (*Fig.* 84). This method, I think, is the most satisfactory and offers more possibility for design expression with infinitely less hazard. In this case the spaces are sawed out instead of being formed by wire. The job of bending the wires and laboriously soldering them into the spaces is thereby obviated. Plan your motif so that no opening is larger than $\frac{3}{16}$ inch in one of its dimensions. For instance, an opening might be $\frac{1}{8}$ inch wide but one inch long or even longer. Careful and accurate sawing with the jeweler's saw is the first requirement. After filing the edges of the sawed-out spaces one may incorporate the filigree technique within the areas if desired. To do this, bands, about 18-gauge wide and as high as the thickness of metal, are soldered into the openings. Tiny bits of hard solder must be employed but care should be taken to remove all solder except that between the joints.

ENAMELING: *Principles and Practice*

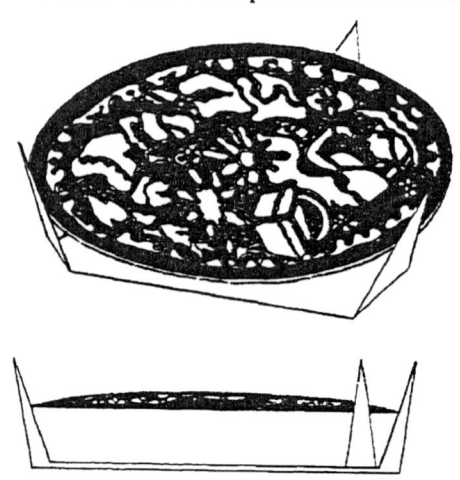

Fig. 84 Method of firing *plique-à-jour* enamels by capillary attraction Place the enamel in the small sawed openings in the metal and suspend the piece on a tripod when firing

APPLYING THE ENAMEL

Now you are ready to apply the enamel Use only your most transparent colors. If you are not positive of the transparency of certain colors, regrind and wash several times or omit the use of such colors entirely. Mix each color with a solution of gum tragacanth, about the consistency of thin mucilage, and place it with the spreader into the openings.

After the piece is fired for the first time, hold it against a strong light. You will find that nearly every small space is completely glassed over. For any spaces which remain unfilled simply proceed with subsequent applications of enamel You should be well rewarded for your efforts, as this technique of enameling is most gratifying. It is seldom seen and offers a wide scope for experimentation. An interesting experiment is to enamel the ordinary $\frac{1}{16}$ inch mesh copper window screening in the *plique-à-jour* manner. Each $\frac{1}{16}$ inch square space holds the enamel by capillary attraction, giving a solid plane of backless transparent color. Such panels inserted into modern lamp shades are both decorative and functional (*Fig.* 85).

Champlevé, Plique-à-jour, Basse-taille and Other Types

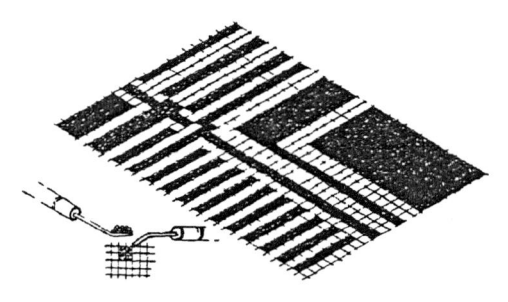

Fig. 85 Plique-à-jour enameling on copper window screening. The enamel is held in the small squares by capillary attraction.

BASSE-TAILLE PROCESS

Another style in enameling is that known as *basse-taille* (*Fig. 86*) in which transparent enamels are fired over a carved metal surface. Procure a piece of fine silver or, better still, a piece of fine gold, which is at least 18-gauge thick. Attach it firmly onto a block of pitch by heating the pitch slightly while the gold

Fig. 86 Basse-taille enameling. Detail of a Fourteenth-Century French reliquary. Here the enamel is placed over a carved background (*Courtesy The Taft Museum, Cincinnati*)

135

ENAMELING: *Principles and Practice*

is in place. Using carving or chasing tools (*Fig.* 87) first carve a rather deep outline around the whole piece and, if desired, around each figure or motif. Refer to your master drawing so that your design is exactly reproduced on the metal. It is advisable to outline the design on the back in an exact duplicate of that on the face Remove the plate from the pitch block in order to do this.

With a hammer or blunt tools raise the design by working from the reverse side. Return to the face of the metal and further develop the design. Carve the metal deeply and refine with a small buffing wheel. Clean and prepare the surface for enameling. Make use of the most delicate layers of well-washed transparent colors. Build up overtones of transparents for blending purposes, enhancing the form already established by the modeling. The deeper engraving around the contour of the figures will give the effect of a strong, dark outline Some opaques may be brought into play for sharper accents. When completed the enamel surface is stoned, giving the smooth, glossy quality of a flawless crystal.

GRISAILLE PROCESS

One may see countless examples of the grisaille type of enameling in many museum collections. It was extensively employed by

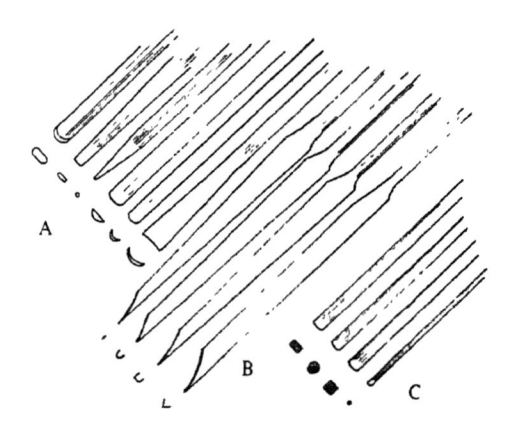

Fig. 87 Tools Used for Carving the Metal in *Basse-taille* Enameling   A. Chasing tools   B. Engraving tools   C. Matting tools.

Champlevé, Plique-à-jour, Basse-taille and Other Types

the Limoges masters (*Fig. 88*). The word grisaille, being derived from the French *gris*, meaning "gray," describes a type of enamel dominantly neutral in color, often made with only black, white and metallic gold. This is an advanced method inasmuch as it involves the knowledge of anatomical structure and three-dimensional representation.

Fig. 88 A Pagan Sacrifice, JEAN POILLEVE, middle of the Sixteenth Century An example of grisaille enameling (*Courtesy Metropolitan Museum of Art*)

First apply a thin coat of black or some reasonably dark enamel to the entire surface. After firing it to a smooth, even coat, draw the composition on the panel with either a pen or No. 00 sable brush, using delicate sketch lines of metallic bright gold. Fire again after you have drawn the design. The lines are only to guide you in developing the forms and will be covered by the first application of white.

You will need a very hard white, sifted and ground to an impalpable state. With a bit of experimenting you will discover the proper dark enamel for the background and the proper white which can be superimposed over it without actually disappearing in its thinnest places. Succeeding coats enable you to "model" with the white, leaving it thicker for the highlights and thinner for the half tones Several firings develop three-dimensional effects as you wish them

Work over the basic modeling with transparent colors. Here, again, it is well to be cautious and add only very thin layers of transparent enamels in order not to lose the anatomy or form. From this point on, further developments, such as the addition of metal foils or liquid metallic colors for accents, may be made wherever the artist desires.

Sometimes only delicate veneers of flux are used over the basic black and white composition, adding, perhaps, a bit of detail work in black overglaze This closely approximates the true grisaille style.

EN RÉSILLE PROCESS

There is another very rare type of enameling called *en résille*. *Résille* is a French word, meaning "hairnet." In appearance the work gives a quality not unlike a delicately woven net. On first glance one might mistake this type of enameling for cloisonné except for the fact that its base is crystal rather than metal. Actually, the delineation producing this exquisite tracery is obtained by the gold outlines of each tiny incised motif.

Because of its rarity and because it represents the ultimate in skill and craftsmanship, I would like to explain further the French *en résille* vanity mirror (*Fig. 89*). It was done in the second half of the Sixteenth Century and purchased in 1926 by the Cleveland Museum of Art. I quote in part from an article by Director Milliken in the Bulletin of that date. "Desire for personal adornment has ever been a powerful incentive to artistic production. Vanity is a peculiarly human failing; but while the women of the Bronze Age were content to use polished metal or the placid surface of a stream to reflect their images, no such humble means could please the 'grandes dames' of the Court of a

Champlevé, Plique-à-jour, Basse-taille and Other Types

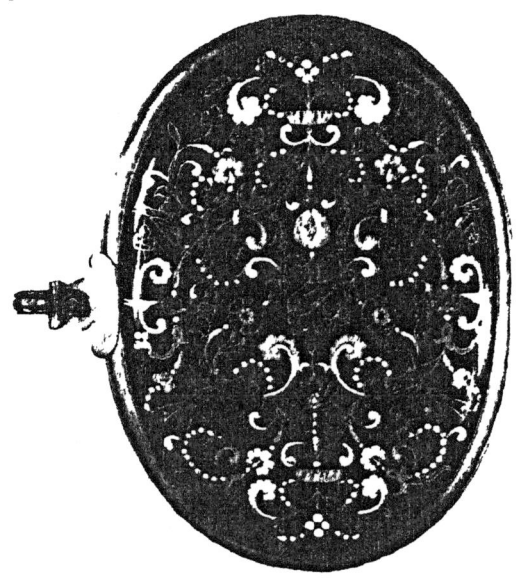

Fig 89 Vanity Mirror, Sixteenth Century An example of *en résille* enameling in which the enamel is placed in small grooves on crystal.

Louis of France The vanity mirrors are but exquisite ancestors of the omnipresent vanity cases of today They are almost nonexistent today. There are two pieces of the "en résille" enamel in the Gallerie d'Apollon in the Louvre, some in the South Kensington Museum, a miniature case in the J. Pierpont Morgan collection and a few examples in private collections. This type of ornamentation, delightful in effect and of a marked delicacy, belongs properly to the French goldsmiths of the second half of the sixteenth century. No one knows to whom the invention of it is due.

"The en résille technique was used for jewelry, for mirror or miniature cases and other objects of adornment. It was indeed a curious technical process. The desired design of arabesques and scrolls was engraved upon the surface of a plaque of glass paste or rock crystal to a depth of perhaps half a millimeter. This incised pattern was then lined with gold and the tiny compartments or cloisons so formed were filled with opaque or trans-

ENAMELING: *Principles and Practice*

lucent enamels of an extreme fusibility [very soft, low-fire colors]. The result, after careful firing and polishing, was a beautiful all-over design almost like a kind of incrustation upon the crystal surface. Needless to say, the process was one of great delicacy, necessarily so because of the excessive fragility of the materials used. The decoration is in the form of a balanced scroll and flower pattern enclosing animal forms, birds and rabbits. The translucent reds, greens and blues are accentuated by opaque whites and yellows with minor touches of pale blue and green."

These, then, constitute the major techniques of enameling listed in the order of their general familiarity: Limoges or painted enamels, cloisonné, champlevé, grisaille, *plique-à-jour, basse-taille* and *en résille* There are variations on these methods and endless opportunities for combining more than one method in a single piece. Today's enamel craftsman will discover that as he tries his hand at each of the styles, it will become so intriguing he will wish for more hours in the day.

IX

DESIGN FOR ENAMELING AND THE UNDERSTANDING AND FEELING FOR THE MEDIUM OF ENAMELING: Scale · Vibration · Edges · Stress · Subject matter

So OFTEN one who acquaints himself with a craft for the purpose of developing a hobby finds that he is hopelessly lost when confronted with the problems of design. It is my belief that he should first have some knowledge of design before attempting any one of the crafts. I do not say that he must have studied design for an accepted number of years, for academic training is not always a criterion for the most talented craftsman. Many of my students have never been exposed to a formal art school training and yet have been able to express themselves admirably in the colorful medium of enameling. The stress, I feel, should be placed upon design theory which is something that can be taught The amateur in his basement workshop will probably come to the realization that a basic knowledge of design is necessary for complete success

I still maintain that enameling may be used as a hobby and is an excellent means of self-expression for novice and professional alike. After all, the words "good design" can be a rather ambiguous term and more often than not it merely implies "good taste." It is not my aim in this chapter to try to teach design. I do, however, propose to discuss it as related to the particular possibilities of enamel on metal.

Before this discussion let me repeat that anyone working in enamels should first develop the complete design in color on paper before attempting it in enamel (*Fig.* 90 A-D). He must try assiduously to match his paints to his enamel tests.

Scale, vibration, edges, stress and subject matter are, in my estimation, important factors of design to discuss in relation to enameling.

ENAMELING: *Principles and Practice*

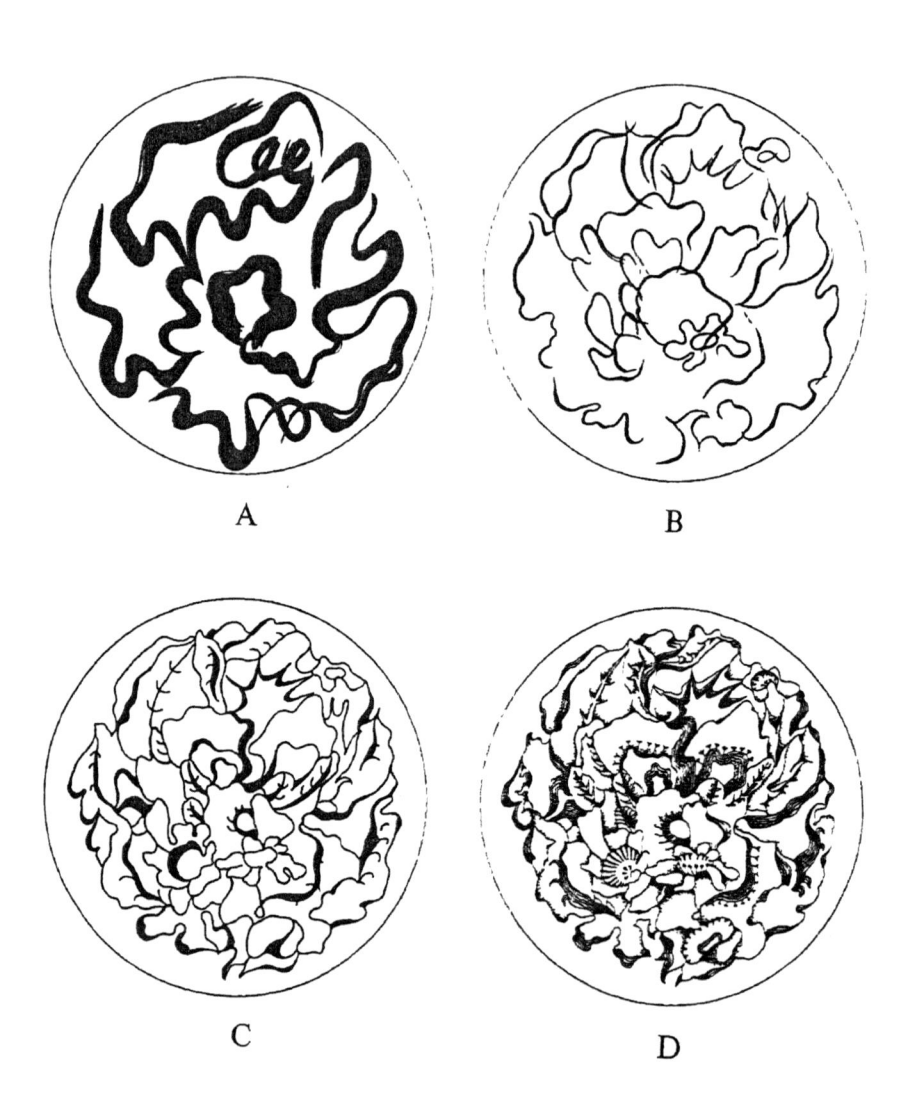

Fig. 90 Creating a Design from Free Brush Strokes   A. Capture certain emotional movements which relate themselves to the given area   B. Develop first abstract brush lines into more conscious or refined shapes   C. Discover meaning to lines, shapes and edges   D. Complete the materialization of the original brush strokes into the intended subject matter.

Design, Understanding and Feeling for Enameling

SCALE

The average distance from which an object will be viewed by the observer determines its scale. This, of course, is a generality and, as such, is subject to many ramifications. But, if this principle is thoughtfully considered before applying a motif to a tray, a decoration to a box, or a border to a bowl, much of the concern with functionalism and appropriateness will be solved automatically. An ash tray is certainly not the appropriate place for a miniature group of figures or a tiny landscape placed in the center These are subjects which demand a larger area. A tray should be so designed that it can be viewed in any position

If, on the other hand, a box or bowl, which is to be viewed from a short distance, has a motif seeming to occupy more than the proper amount of space, it is also wrong in scale. It is oversized while the first was undersized. Neither is functional nor appropriate for the piece of enamel that was chosen to be executed In *Hibiscus Flower (Fig* 39C) one bloom occupies completely the twelve-inch plate which is justified only on the basis that it is intended for a shelf decoration in a dining room where it would never be seen at a range of less than six to eight feet

What is meant when we criticize the design as being uninterestingly plain and unbroken in some of its areas? The error is with the scale of the objects chosen which gives a sense of emptiness to the entire composition. This does not preclude such a composition provided the spaces and shapes are so constructed that they attract the viewer's interest. A design that is said to be too "busy," meaning it contains too many small broken areas, could again be due to a lack of judgment in scale. I have discussed the matter of scale first, because it is so often the cause of poorly designed enameled objects. The relation of the size of a motif or decoration to the size of the object to receive it must be considered throughout the execution of the piece.

VIBRATION

In no other medium, unless it is stained glass, must the artist be more cognizant of the function of vibrating colors than in enamel work Its misuse is second in the list of causes for poor design. The dictionaries describe vibration as an oscillating or quivering motion With flat or mat-finished colors one may create vibrations with certain juxtapositions of opposite hues or close dissonances, but with glossy-surfaced colors the vibratory effect is enhanced In enamels there are no dull or mat finishes The opaque colors have a varnishlike surface and the transparent enamels over silver or gold foil have even more brilliancy plus depth. The juxtaposition of one strongly colored transparent enamel and one brilliant opaque can set up an unpleasant vibration if not judiciously chosen. A major difficulty and, often, the cause of crude color effects is the superfluous use of shimmering colors applied over metal foils This blatant and gaudy quality can be avoided if the designer will curb his desire to overuse these brilliant color accents It is a natural temptation to be attracted by the glitter of highly polished metal or enamel surfaces. How often I have seen the beginning student in metalcraft forget previous training in design when attempting his first silver finger ring! This, I find, is true also of the beginner in enameling, and not until he corrects the major error of excessive use of highly vibrating colors does he achieve a well-balanced design.

In the cloisonné and champlevé processes one is constantly playing the polished, exposed metal against the brilliancy of the enamels. Caution must be exercised in order not to let one brilliant surface overbalance the other It is a good plan to use opaque colors in cloisonné and champlevé work for technical reasons as well as for the aesthetic reasons mentioned above Oxidation of the exposed metal is one way of subordinating it to the importance of the enamel.

EDGES

With most mediums — such as oil painting, water color, charcoal drawings or block printing, the edge, whether direct or indirect is always controlled by the tool. In the case of enameling, however, the edge created by the tool is subject to variations

Design, Understanding and Feeling for Enameling

caused by the action of heat on the glaze. Unless firing conditions are well understood, the character may be lost in the firing operation and edges inappropriate to the design may result For example, *Kilarney, Ontario* (*Fig* 91) shows a subject treated in a purely geometric manner. The intention was to interpret the wharf, buildings and gulls with stiff edges and to keep the deliberately planned triangles and lines in place with almost mechanical precision. The edges here are all-important and necessitate a firing temperature that controls their exact positions, not allowing for freedom or discrepancies.

In the majority of cases, the enamelist is not so concerned with the stiff edge as with a free, flowing edge. The charm of enamels is partly dependent upon the character of edges, and a certain quality of design can be tangibly achieved through their control. Try the experiment of placing transparent ruby red next to flux in an inlaid pattern Fire the enamel at 1550° F. and observe

Fig. 91 Kilarney, Ontario, KENNETH F. BATES, 1946. The geometric interpretation requires low firing in order to keep colors and shapes in their exact positions.

ENAMELING: *Principles and Practice*

the resulting edges The ruby red fires to a dark maroon over copper and seems to bleed into the flux. leaving an intense halation of claret-wine color. Such an edge cannot be achieved in the medium of painting and is caused only by the fluid quality of enamel glazes when subjected to heat. Opaque red leaves a peculiar black edge and soft opaque pinks seem to ooze into the adjoining color When the enamelist has learned the characteristics of each of his fired colors. he will realize the value of edges and be able to utilize them In *Gloxinias (Fig 92)* a pale-green edge to the leaves and stems was intentionally planned by firing a hard transparent over a soft opaque enamel.

Fig. 92 Gloxinias, KENNETH F. BATES, 1939. An enameled plate which demonstrates the use of diffused edges as seen around the leaves and stems. (*Courtesy Cleveland Museum of Art*)

Design, Understanding and Feeling for Enameling

The overfiring of enamels causes sharp edges to become obliterated. Original designs when laid on with the spatula are sometimes sacrificed, but the result often surpasses a too consciously planned pattern. *Experiment 9B (Fig* 39D), an example of overfiring, shows a composition of simple flower forms with petals radiating from a center When the enamel was applied the petals were straight and certainly less interesting than the effect shown. Notice that the petals have become wavy and edges are quite free. Further overfiring brings about even more distortion

The stiffness of edge produced by the stencil method in enameling has its disadvantages Combining a stenciled edge with areas having diffused edges gives a more satisfactory and, in my opinion, a more contemporary quality to the design

STRESS

By the word "stress" in regard to design theory, I do not mean emphasis alone Stress implies dynamic pull in one direction or a series of directions. Pulls in one direction must, in turn, be counterbalanced by the same amount of stress in the opposite direction. Allen Tucker in his treatise *Design and the Idea* states that "it is hard to live with things which are out of balance .. unbalance gives a feeling of distress to everyone." There are endless means by which balance within a circular, square or rectangular composition can be achieved, but none is more vital than the study of stresses, or directionalism, brought about through line, shape and color.

Referring again to *Kilarney, Ontario (Fig.* 91), it will be noticed that as one large gull flies out of the circular composition to the left, several fly into the picture. It is of greater importance to direct stresses toward the subject than away from it. The sails represented abstractly by triangles pointing up and out of the plate would, if not checked, lead the eye out of the composition at the top. To oppose this vertical stress, horizontal cloud shapes and gulls flying in an exact countermovement were added (*Fig.* 93). I doubt if any artist is concerned with these theories while he is developing his design to the extent that the foregoing analy-

ENAMELING: *Principles and Practice*

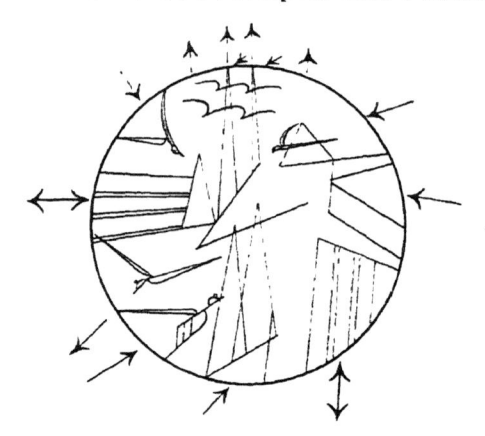

Fig 93 Diagram showing by direction of arrows the movement and countermovement within the composition *Kilarney, Ontario.*

sis implies. However, he undoubtedly utilizes certain theoretical principles of balance previously proven satisfactory to him.

At the risk of being accused of pedantry, I refer to one more of my own compositions which is less obvious in the study of stresses but which may serve to clarify my point further. *Jungle Rhythms* (*Fig.* 94) was intended to create the feeling of more or less chaotic entanglement of tropical growth. However, the final result, which is confined within a square, proposes to portray chaos by relating the stresses to that given area It is a kind of ordered disorder, related to the square area.

The diagram (*Fig.* 95) shows the relationship of major stresses to minor stresses. Shapes such as leaves and petals direct the eye by their contours as well as by their axes. Lines through the centers of small spots create the movement which must be related to other lines regardless of the shape of the spots themselves.

Whether the movement is carried out of the picture or kept within is of less concern than the control of stresses which, in the final analysis, must present a plausible feeling of balance. The theory that every successful design is balanced would, indeed, not be a dangerous premise, so diversified and numerous are the means of achieving this end. The main point is that by the control

Design, Understanding and Feeling for Enameling

Fig. 94 Jungle Rhythms, KENNETH F. BATES, 1947. An enameled composition designed to show the chaotic movements of tropical growth.

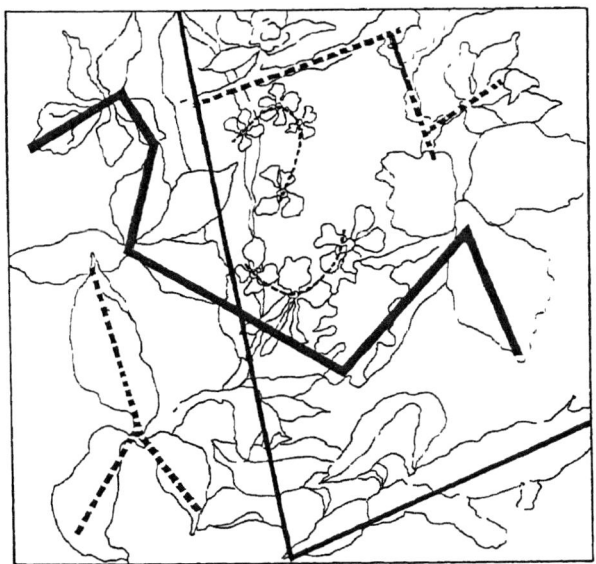

Fig. 95 An analysis of *Jungle Rhythms.* The heaviest solid line designates the direction of the main movement. Secondary movements are shown by the thinner line and the dotted lines.

of stresses within, or outside of, a composition, the artist consciously balances every design he makes whether in enamel or any other medium.

SUBJECT MATTER

The fact that the creative artist may express himself successfully in one medium does not predestine his success in another. The peculiarities of enamel are such that certain processes put limitations on the type of subject matter which can be used. As stated before much depends on the fusibility of the colors and on the time it takes the differently compounded enamels to reach their maturity in firing.

For a beginner I would recommend an abstract or purely nonobjective approach, playing more with color juxtapositions and proportionate areas and shapes than with any specific theme I think this suggestion is a valid one even though good nonobjective or abstract compositions are not merely beginner's luck. The enamelist does, however, need to experiment with more than one type of enameling before he is adequately prepared with enough techniques to allow subject matter to dominate his thinking Subjects dealing with fine lines or thin, narrow bands of color are not as appropriate for the inlaid technique as for the cloisonné or painted enamel Such rules are learned only by practical application. To emphasize a free organic line requires the use of a different method as can be seen in *Delineation* (Fig. 96). Here a practically solid area of opaque turquoise enamel was applied as a base and after a few pieces of wet string were arranged on the panel, black enamel was dusted over the entire surface. Removing the string caused the pattern to appear. This design could not have been so freely expressed by any other approach without certain technical difficulties.

"What to render" in enamel need not be a stumbling block for the student—"how to render" is of greater importance. There is not space enough here to discuss completely the inspirational sources for artists in enamel.

Abstract and geometric types of design have already been

Design, Understanding and Feeling for Enameling

Fig. 96 Delineation, KENNETH F BATES, 1950. An approach to design by means of line alone.

mentioned. Nature—plants, flowers, birds, marine life, etc.—never disappoints the artist as a source of design. Look on the back of fern leaves, for example, and discover the spores arranged in patterns and series. *Sporangia (Fig 97)* shows how well ferns lend themselves to the medium of enamel. Notice that the enamel was applied in tiny pearl-like drops to simulate the spores on the leaves. Whether one prefers an abstract, stylized (*Fig.* 98) or naturalistic interpretation is immaterial. Inspiration for enameling will be found everywhere in nature, from the most microscopic animal to the mountains in all their grandeur.

Often subject matter is near at hand, in the studio or just outside the window, *Spring Comes in My Window (Fig. 99).* Here, again, the inspiration must be translated in the mind of the

Fig. 97 Sporangia, KENNETH F. BATES, 1945. Spores on the backs of fern leaves serve as an appropriate use for small white drops of enamels.

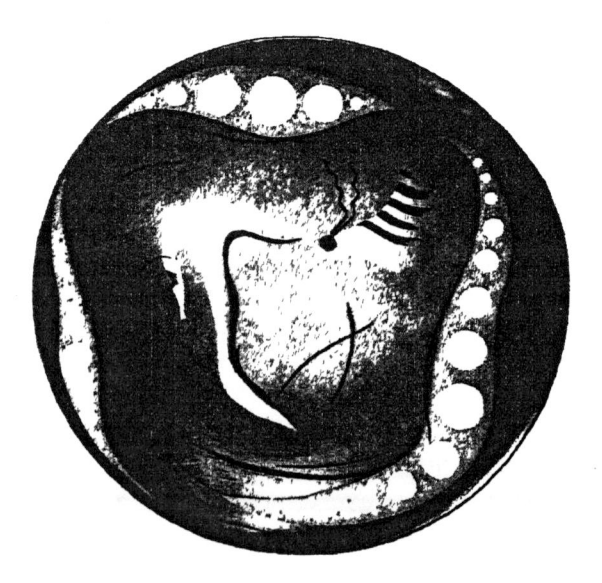

Fig. 98 The Chase, KENNETH F. BATES, 1948. Inspiration may always be found in nature although the result may become highly stylized.

Design, Understanding and Feeling for Enameling

Fig. 99 Spring Comes in My Window, KENNETH F. BATES, 1949.

enamelist in terms of a style which is compatible and complementary to the idea. It is not enough to duplicate the flash of color or exciting play of textures which occur, without serious consideration for their functional applications. Still-life subjects can also be interpreted in enamels (*Fig. 100*).

Not unlike the painter in oils or water colors, the enamel craftsman discovers that scenery, places and faces are forever suggesting subject matter for his medium. The kaleidoscopic patterns at the market place, the county fair or crowded railway station are viewed as possible subjects, because the broken areas of color lend themselves superbly to this medium.

My Trip to Pittsburgh (*Fig.* 101) shows the results of interpreting a given locality in the medium of enamel. It has an advantage over most mediums inasmuch as it can literally resort to depths of color and metallic brightness.

ENAMELING. *Principles and Practice*

Fig. 100 *Flower Arrangement,* KENNETH F. BATES, 1950. The arrangement of still life and flowers is accumulative in the artist's mind rather than a consciously planned "set-up" of the moment.

Fig. 101 *My Trip to Pittsburgh,* KENNETH F. BATES, 1948.

Design, Understanding and Feeling for Enameling

Subject matter which is dictated by a specific purpose, such as ecclesiastical subjects, have greater limitations for the designer. Restrictions are always imposed regarding the interpretation of Biblical characterizations (*Fig* 102). These restrictions are set up by rubrical authorities and very little divergence from the established ritual can be abrogated.

Ecclesiastical art deserves some degree of conviction, or at least respect, on the part of the artist, and most assuredly on the part of the artist in enamel. The result must be dignified and spiritual in tone.

As the history of enameling deals so largely with masterpieces made for the church I feel that here is a field for the enamelist

Fig. 102 *Stations of the Cross,* KENNETH F. BATES, 1944. The religious narrative must be carefully followed.

ENAMELING: *Principles and Practice*

of today which has hardly been touched. The chalice, pyx, triptych or enameled picture present excellent opportunities for the modern enamel craftsman *(Fig. 103)*

These various suggestions for subject matter are offered only as an incentive to those who have not realized the magnitude of the medium. Considering all the ways in which enamel can be applied, the possible effects and techniques, there is no type of subject matter which could not be successfully reproduced in some way or another

A sense of depth in color could be proposed as the most outstanding characteristic of enamels. Jewel-like quality and the play of broken color are of equal importance. Without a sincere recognition of these qualities, the enamelist is apt to miss the unique characteristics of the medium.

Fig. 103 A group of ecclesiastical enamels, KENNETH F. BATES, 1934. Ecclesiastical interpretation requires dignified handling Following are design ideas appropriate for the medium of enameling from simple to more complex motifs.

156

Design, Understanding and Feeling for Enameling

A. One color motif

B. Two color line motif

C. Line and mass motif

D. Three value geometric motif

E. Simple stencil motif

F. Flat areas with texture

ENAMELING: *Principles and Practice*

G Textures, line and mass

H. Simple animal motif

I. Two-dimensional flowers

J. Still life

K. Stencil and foil motif

L. Leaves

158

Design, Understanding and Feeling for Enameling

M. Masquerade

N. Spot, line and mass

O. Bird motif

P. Figures

Q. Fish motif

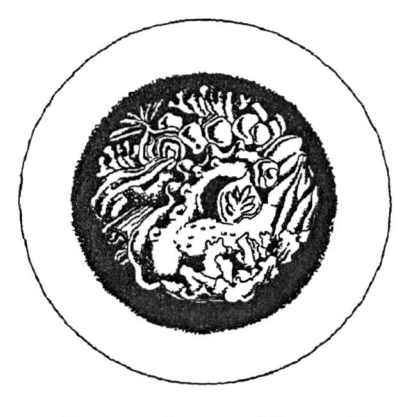

R. Fruit and vegetable motif.

X

EXPERIMENTS, SUGGESTIONS FOR NEW USES OF ENAMEL AND EARNING A LIVING BY ENAMELING: EXPERIMENT 1 – Enameled jewels · EXPERIMENT 2 – Gas flame colorations · EXPERIMENT 3 – Enameling over fireglaze · EXPERIMENT 4 – Overglaze shading · EXPERIMENT 5 – The thin enameled line · EXPERIMENT 6 – The embossed line · EXPERIMENT 7 – Sgraffito technique · EXPERIMENT 8 – Enameling on brass · EXPERIMENT 9 – Textures with glass

EXPERIMENTATION and the resulting discoveries along any line of endeavor are bound to be very personal. The temptation to hold on to such "finds" and dream of making a fortune, or of living in a Utopian existence where only you know the secret is not uncommon. As an instructor in an art school, where both student and leader find themselves rather humbled before an erstwhile noble craft, I became aware that such covetous thoughts were soon dissipated. In the classroom the instructor will admit, if he is honest with himself, that he generally receives more than he gives. In the studio, having made discoveries which are not applicable to the pedagogical routine, he has a tendency to forget the reciprocity he owes his students. Some of my studio experiments have been kept for a period of years and, with the thought of helping other enamelists who have been an inspiration to me, I now wish to record the following experiments for what they may be worth.

EXPERIMENT 1: *Enameled jewels*

Once, while visiting the studio of Charles Mosgo, a potter, I

Experiments, Suggestions for New Uses of Enamel

noticed that, occasionally, glazes which had been applied to ceramics would become molten to the point of liquefaction, causing them to run off the clay forms and drop to the floor of the kiln. These driblets were extremely enchanting, having qualities not unlike rare jewels or scarce matrices I have always been fascinated with the marbleized appearance of glazes Perhaps many of us remember being possessive about our childhood collection of marbles. With such memories, plus the new incentive of the pottery glaze driblets, I proceeded to find a way of producing the same result with enamels. Actually, as it developed, the experiment resulted in something quite simple and obvious but was, nevertheless, of use in creating new effects.

This is the way it can be done With a small hammer break up chunks of enamel frit, preferably the most glassy hard transparents, such as gold, yellow, aquamarine or sapphire. Also try hard white, beige and pink opaques. Place a variety of sizes on a charcoal block and play the blowtorch directly on them. The flame must be continuous and never replaced once it is withdrawn from the enamel. The result will be a spherical shape slightly flattened at the base.

By making many of these "jewels" it is possible to obtain a number of them that are the same size or they can be made in different sizes and arranged according to the requirements of your design. To carry the enamel "jewel" a step further in brilliancy, punch tiny circles of silver or gold foil with a harness punch, place between two chunks of the unground enamel and fire. The pure metal foil becomes imbedded in the jewel, causing an intense sparkle One can readily see that their uses are numerous. Keep a supply of them in various colors and stages of opacity for supplementing enameled jewelry.

Apply the "jewels" to an already enameled surface by picking them up with pointed jeweler's tweezers and dipping them in a thick solution of gum tragacanth. Place them flat side down. By carefully drying them before firing, the exact position can be retained while fusing in the kiln Watch the firing closely to determine the way they become joined to the basic enamel. You may adhere them slightly by a gentle firing or obtain a hobnail

ENAMELING: *Principles and Practice*

Fig. 104 Small pillbox, KENNETH F. BATES, 1946 An example of the use of enameled "jewels" as described in Experiment 1

glass effect by longer fusing in the kiln.

I have used these "jewels" in costume earrings, brooches, pins, hair ornaments and small pillboxes (*Fig.* 104). This idea can be further developed by the resourceful designer as it presents unlimited possibilities.

EXPERIMENT 2: *Gas flame colorations*

Perhaps without the use of the electric kiln one might come upon many unique characteristics of enamel. It is certain that when I had only the gas blowtorch in the first years of my work, I could observe chemical changes and also watch the fusibility of each enamel as it melted. Watchful study of this kind is not possible while the piece is being fired in the kiln and undoubtedly one misses much which might be of value.

While making small plaques to be set into a composite box (*Fig.* 105), using the mouth blowtorch as a firing instrument, I took precautions to keep the flame constantly dispersed by a wire mesh but, by accident, allowed it to hit the surface of the enamel. I was amazed to find, when the enamel cooled, that a most striking gold patina, or film, had been deposited on the

Experiments, Suggestions for New Uses of Enamel

Fig. 105 Small silver box, KENNETH F. BATES, 1930 Enamel panels, one square inch in size, were made without the use of an enameling kiln. Many interesting effects can be achieved by firing with the blowtorch as described in Experiment 2.

enamel I now realize that my discovery was not new; in fact, various patinas were formed in much the same way by Chinese makers of pottery and porcelain.

To be a little more explicit, first use a dark transparent, such as cobalt or dark brown. After the enamel has been thoroughly matured the direct flame should be passed over it Let the red, or point, part of a large flame play upon one side of the enamel for a moment and quickly withdraw it. In more scientific terms, one is deoxidizing the enamel glaze, bringing it to a metallic state by a reduction flame, thereby removing nonmetallic elements. On small pieces which can be produced with the blowtorch method of firing, this experiment offers an opportunity for unusual effects.

EXPERIMENT 3: *Enameling over fire glaze*

After much exacting and careful instruction regarding the various methods of cleaning copper in preparation for enameling, the student is rather dismayed to find that he is able to enamel directly over fire glaze with no cleaning whatsoever. It was some

ENAMELING. *Principles and Practice*

time before I discovered that burned and overfired edges of trays could be successfully re-enameled without removing the fire glaze.

On a large surface one may first create the fire glaze by bringing the copper to a red heat (about 1500° F) and allowing it to form by retaining the above heat for three to four minutes. Remove the plate and immerse in cold water Usually, the fire glaze cracks off in places, leaving interesting patches of copper in completely free organic or geometric shapes Rub the piece with a fine emery cloth or give it a quick dip in a dilute nitric-acid bath, but only enough to clean the exposed copper patches.

This may now be enameled for use as a textured background, cloud or underwater effects, or any other abstract basis for developing your design motifs I find that the fire glaze does not chip off once it has been enameled. Flux and transparent beige, especially, give a rich quality which is worthy of notice.

EXPERIMENT 4: *Overglaze shading*

For work which requires detail or even the bolder abstract type of motif which demands some three-dimensional exaggeration, overglaze shading offers the best solution. It is absolutely essential, however, that one has a clear understanding of the term "overglaze enamel paintings " Actually, there are two distinct types of this kind of enamel, the "vitrified" and the "vitrifiable." Vitrified colors have been previously melted and dissolved into a flux and are essentially like any enamel except that they are much finer and have about ten times as much coloring matter. Vitrifiable colors are merely oxides which are mixed with finely ground flux and become united only after they are fired. The vitrified colors have a certain depth and brilliancy and are manufactured in both the opaque and transparent state. The vitrifiable colors, on the other hand, are quite easy to manage with a brush and include the well-known china-painting colors. Many sets of these colors, left over from the china-painting vogue of the early 1900's, have been given to me. They were the instigation for my experiments with vitrifiable colors.

Experiments, Suggestions for New Uses of Enamel

It is well to regrind the amount of color needed each time. Place a small amount of the powdered color on a heavy glass slab together with the quantity of oils needed for manageability, and grind it to an impalpable state with a flexible palette knife.

I find that there are many choices for a vehicle to use in overpainting My own choice is oil of lavender or oil of sassafras (synthetic oils work as well as the genuine) and a drop of squeegee oil used as a binder Both of these vehicles are entirely volatile, in other words, readily vaporizable, leaving no trace or discoloration on the enamel. For accurate control of the medium, apply the enamel with either a fine No 00 sable brush or pen point. A little more of the vehicle placed beside an area will allow one to shade the colors (*Fig.* 106). For this, employ an ordinary stippling brush or a water-color brush with the bristles cut off at the end

Fig. 106 *Big Top Celebrities,* KENNETH F. BATES, 1948. It is possible to shade the overglaze colors with oil as shown in the features of the two clowns.

ENAMELING: *Principles and Practice*

An important precautionary step is thorough drying Dry the piece over a low heat until all of the oil has been dissipated, leaving a lighter colored powdery surface before fusing. Do not try to paint heavily with either the vitrified or vitrifiable colors. A more judicious procedure is to apply several thin washes with separate firings. These delicate layers of color obviously need less heat than ordinary enamels so it is wise to fire gently (from $1000°$ F. to $1300°$ F), bringing the basic enamel back together after it has cracked.

Blending, sgraffito, thin water-color effects, and cross-hatching are only a few ways in which this medium can be treated. There is no limit to the possibilities of overpainting, although I do not feel that it has very much of the true enamel quality.

EXPERIMENT 5: *The thin enameled line*

This experiment, I have found, is one which has been used commercially for some time.

To create hair-thin lines in enamel is very difficult with the usual processes already mentioned. For a more permanent and richer line of any width, first draw the intended linear design with a pen point, using squeegee oil or any volatile oil having the proper viscidity and thickness to it The oil will remain moist for some time and this is important in performing the next step. A small sieve is improvised with fine silk stretched across it. This silk should be at least 120 mesh or even finer. Scatter or dust the desired color from the sieve over the entire enamel surface until the oil lines are covered up and all oil is absorbed. Now blow off any fine dust which is not stuck to the oil line and you are ready to place the piece in the kiln. In firing, do not use too much heat or the lines may spread, spoiling the delicate linear pattern. Lettering, mechanical lines, highlights and scientific drawings are possible with such a technique. If the dusting leaves an indistinct line, repeat the process until the proper value is attained.

EXPERIMENT 6: *The embossed line*

There are times when a variation of surface improves the

Experiments, Suggestions for New Uses of Enamel

character of an entire design, even though the level, stoned surface is the more legitimate. When variations in the thicknesses of enamels are caused by haphazard planning or without deliberate intent, the effect is anything but professional and the resulting highlights on each mound or irregular surface become confusing to the eye But if the raised line or area is an integral part of the design it can be most effective. To be more explicit, suppose marine life, undersea plants and coral formations were chosen as a subject for enameling (*Fig.* 107). The whole treatment could be enhanced if the fan-shaped coral were introduced as an embossed or raised motif. The coral, being composed of a network of narrow, crossing lines, gives a very decorative effect, whether treated abstractly or naturalistically.

Fig. 107 *Marine Fantasy,* KENNETH F. BATES, 1948. The embossed line, as described in Experiment 6, was used for the light-colored coral in the foreground.

ENAMELING: *Principles and Practice*

To render the coral in a raised pattern, first choose an extremely hard, or high-fire, enamel The hard dial white, hard beige or a hard yellow opaque will suffice. Mix a small amount of the opaque enamel, after sifting it through 100-mesh screening, with a thick, concentrated solution of gum tragacanth, making a heavy paste Now with the spatula in the left hand and the spreader in the right, hold a small globule of the moist color on the spatula close to the enameled plate. Push off the enamel with the spreader to form "paths," or lines, of color, thus creating the coral pattern. Heap the enamel high, at least $\frac{1}{16}$ inch, as it will be held in place while firing by the gum tragacanth. We now have a hard enamel in an extra-thick application. Fire until the surface of the coral has just become molten and then withdraw from the kiln.

The effect will be like that of the old Wedgwood pottery—an embossed motif on a flat surface. I have used the coral as perhaps a rather obvious example to explain this experiment, but I leave it to others to make adaptations of this unique effect in enamel.

EXPERIMENT 7: *Sgraffito technique*

The most attractive examples of subtle linear motifs are often rendered in what might be termed "enamel sgraffito." Choose a large bowl or plate for this experiment in order to give free play to a spontaneous and moving line. First, I suggest making numerous actual-sized, freehand drawings, getting the "feel" of the shape to be decorated and the sense of its proportions Use the hard line made by a pencil or the flexible line of a brush for this preliminary work as the sgraffito can be worked in either a solid or shaded line. In any case, as the final drawings must be made rapidly in order to capture a sense of freedom and rhythm, preliminary sketching is a great help All voluntary action is lost when the line is laboriously traced.

Almost any combination of transparent or opaque enamels can be used for the sgraffito work, but some are more applicable than others. Try a base coat of flux, covering the plate completely and firing to a brilliant, transparent flesh color. Now with opaque

Experiments, Suggestions for New Uses of Enamel

turquoise, browns, reds, beige or black, dust in free areas or masses with the silk sieve or fine wire mesh, letting some sense of pattern guide the distribution In this experiment, the opaques are dusted just heavy enough to cover the surface in the important areas and blended together or faded out as one wishes. Spray the whole surface with a medium-thick tragacanth solution. This is necessary to hold the separated particles in place on the second firing. With the blunt end of a paintbrush or with the pointer, draw in your line pattern briskly and freshly, keeping in mind the relationship of lines to the colored opaque areas Fire high enough to cause the undercoat of flux to flow slightly.

A variation, which has proven successful, is to employ a dark-blue or black opaque for the base coat and superimpose a fairly complete layer of opaque ivory. While the ivory coat is slightly damp, draw the line of the design with the tip of the spreader. As the spreader point is pulled along through the ivory area it should leave an interesting feathered track (*Fig.* 108)

EXPERIMENT 8: *Enameling on brass*

Many craftsmen ask if enamels will adhere to brass. For all practical purposes the answer is "no." However, I shall describe an experiment which took place in my classroom involving research by a probing student who was as cognizant as I of the fact that many of the Chinese and some of the early French enamels were done on brass. Possibly by accident, a piece of soft rolled brass which had been previously etched for champlevé work was placed in the kiln and heated to about 1450° F. The brass was then removed from the kiln, and a blackish fire glaze formed over the entire surface. This was not removed, as in the case of cleaning other metals for enameling, but simply wiped with a soft cloth to remove the more flaky parts. The brass was then enameled in the small recessed areas of the champlevé design. The perfect adherence of the enamel to the brass was a surprising, new experience for both instructor and student. Heretofore, after preparing brass in the usual cleaning method with acid and steel wool, enamel had refused to hold while cooling.

ENAMELING: *Principles and Practice*

Fig 108 *Arabesque*, KENNETH F. BATES, 1948. The sgraffito technique, as described in Experiment 7, was used on the left of this twelve-inch plate

It would fly from the brass in large flakes, an experience which is only too familiar to those who have tried to enamel on this metal.

Analyzing the procedure of the experiment, it will be noted that the brass was annealed and allowed to oxidize, or form fire glaze, before enameling. Brass is an alloy of copper with a large percentage of zinc and, often, tin added. These alloys have a tendency to burn out, or come to the surface in the form of oxidization. Note also that the blackish ash, or oxidized alloy, was only casually wiped away with a rag. In the original state, before annealing the brass, the alloys are not brought to the surface and any cleaning or polishing only lessens the chance of adhesion with the enamel.

Only opaque enamels are advisable for brass. Transparent enamels can be used, but since they are applied over a dull

Experiments, Suggestions for New Uses of Enamel

surface of fire glaze no real transparent quality should be anticipated.

EXPERIMENT 9: *Textures with glass*

The fusible and elastic characteristics of glass make it an attractive vehicle for studio experimentation (*Fig.* 109). There is never a dearth of spellbound onlookers in the glass blower's tent at a county fair Color transparency and light reflections hold the attention of all This same fascination prompted the following experiments in adding sparkle to the surface of enamels in the way of textures.

For example, after firing an even coat of transparent sapphire on copper I developed a motif in opaque white and some darker transparent blues Then, by way of textural relief, related areas, or spots, cut from white woven glass textile were introduced. The glass cloth is made by the yard for drapery and upholstery material or is sometimes used as belts for machinery. Being composed entirely of threads of glass, it adhered perfectly to the undercoat of enamel Over this woven texture—frayed ends or separate

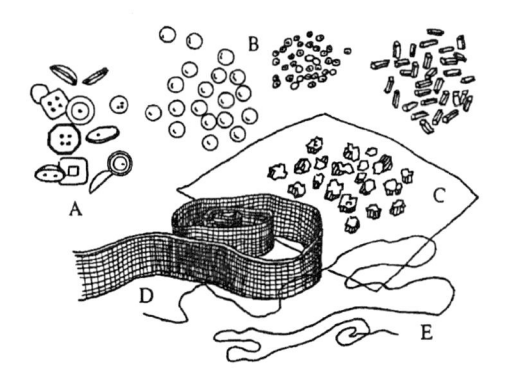

Fig. 109 As described in Experiment 9 various glass objects may be adapted to the enamel surface for variety in texture A. Glass buttons B. Glass beads and balls C. Chunks of enamel frit D. Woven glass cloth E. Fiber from glass cloth can be used for thin lines.

ENAMELING: *Principles and Practice*

threads may be employed, also—I placed a thin coat of pale transparent turquoise, completing the cold color scheme The result was an enamel with the surface texture of cloth.

Glass beads of every description will also give texture variations Chunks of unground enamels, crushed marbles or glass buttons all seem rather illegitimate in the traditional sense, but if the present generation is to carry the art of enameling beyond its former development, there must be no hidebound restrictions placed upon the studio adventurer Enameling should be considered no more static as a vehicle for art expression than any other medium. The nine experiments listed above may open new vistas for the creative artist.

SUGGESTIONS FOR NEW USES OF ENAMEL

A few suggestions for enameled objects less often seen follow

1 Small silver goblets for serving wine or cocktails with *plique-à-jour* insets (*Fig* 110). The *plique-à-jour* enamel is suggested as a separate unit set with a bezel, allowing the goblet to be made of sterling silver instead of fine silver Enameling is more successful on the fine silver, but the sterling is more practical for the goblet

2 A modern wall or studio light incorporating co-ordinated geometric forms (*Fig* 111). The light might have large panels up to six square inches made by the *plique-à-jour* technique of

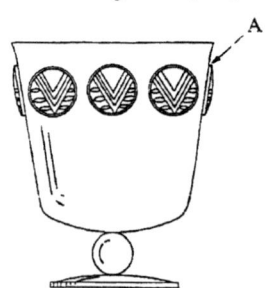

Fig. 110 A small sterling silver cocktail goblet showing the use of *plique-à-jour* insets   A   Each enamel is set with a fine silver bezel.

Experiments, Suggestions for New Uses of Enamel

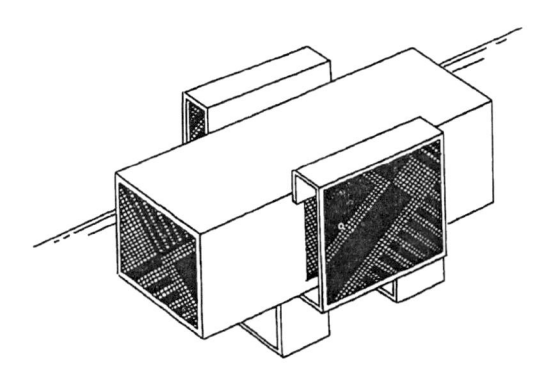

Fig 111 A modern wall or studio light could be made using the *plique-à-jour* enamel on copper window screening for the transparent openings

enameling with ordinary $\frac{1}{16}$ inch mesh copper screening. The enamel holds to the wire screening in the same way that it does to cloisons. Fire the *plique-à-jour* panel on sheets of mica filling each square hole with enamel. By capillary attraction each opening retains the enamel and it is possible to complete the panel in two firings.

3 Demitasse spoons using champlevé or *plique-à-jour* enamel on the handles. The spoons may be plated with silver or gold after enameling and not affect the enamel. Guard against the very soft opaque colors The bowl of the spoon could be enameled, also, or kept plain.

4 Enameled bracelet and matching finger ring (*Fig. 112*). The bracelet may be composed of rectangular panels linked together through a series of holes left in the ends. Use sterling silver for the links and fine silver for the panels. In order to facilitate firing the panels so that no enamel touches the kiln (counterenamel must be used), improvise a kind of clothesline upon which the panels may be strung. Two standards of stainless steel with a piece of Nicrome wire suspended between them will enable you to "hang" the panels without any part of the enamel touching the kiln.

The finger ring could be made of an unsoldered band of

ENAMELING: *Principles and Practice*

copper, such as a slice from copper tubing. If solder must be used, only the hardest hard solder is practical for enameling. The band ring must be fired first in one position and then in another to keep the enamel from running to one side

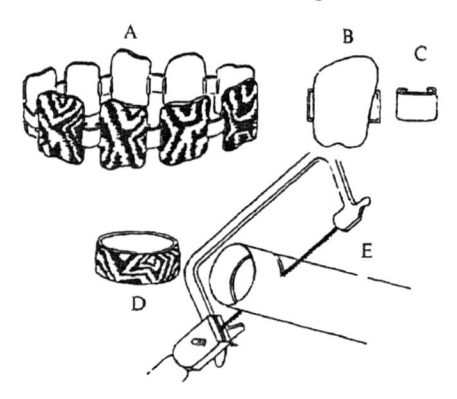

Fig. 112 A Simple enameled links for a bracelet B Extend the metal slots beyond the enameled area C The links are of silver D. Enamel the entire band ring E. Saw the band ring from a tube of metal.

5. Using the enameled jewels as described in this chapter, make a small pillbox for a lady's purse or a stamp box. The entire project can be done with the blowtorch as it involves enameling on a small scale Heap the jewels together to create a brilliant and sparkling effect (*Fig.* 104).

6. The steel panels used for doors or sections of commercially enameled gas ranges are excellent for pictures or wall plaques. They may be set in series for a wall decoration. The white opaque enamel as applied and fired on these plaques by the manufacturer is not unlike the Limoges ground coat and presents an inspiring opportunity for colored compositions. The transparent enamels, if dusted lightly, seem to have a special quality over the dead white ground. Glowing areas and details are readily achieved with the silver foil paillons. These steel plaques will warp in firing but usually return to their normal shape when cool. For most commercial purposes the panels are cast, or pressed down, at their edges, having a depth of ·¾ inch. Such a formed piece of

Experiments, Suggestions for New Uses of Enamel

steel maintains its shape after innumerable firings and is not subject to cracking. Small bathroom or kitchen enameled tiles may be used in the same way. *Midsummer Night* (*Fig.* 113) is an example of enameling on a steel panel.

EARNING A LIVING BY ENAMELING

It is entirely gratifying to an instructor to observe the results of his efforts in the accomplishments of his most successful students That he may open certain doors for further study or suggest untried vistas for experimentation is any teacher's aim. But in the case of enameling the teacher may be doubly rewarded to discover that his students are not only able to find self-expression, but also to use it as a means of earning a living.

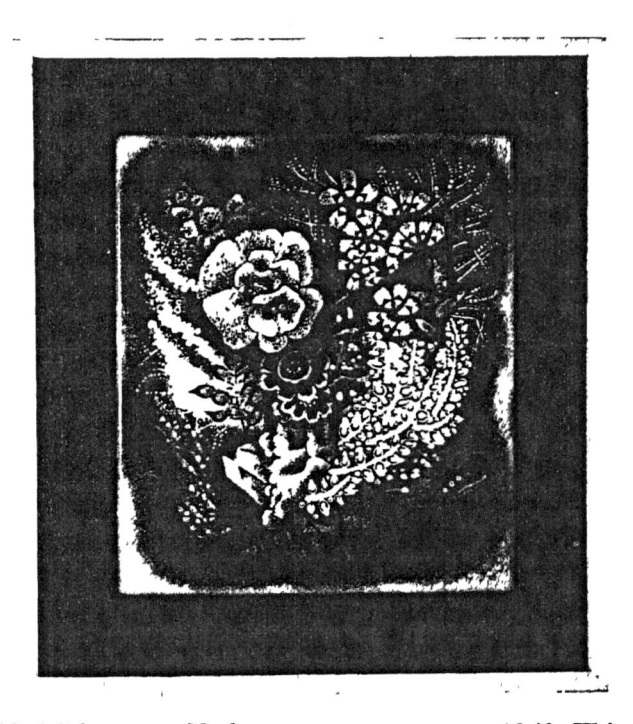

Fig 113 *Midsummer Night*, KENNETH F. BATES, 1949. This enameled panel was made on a steel plate which was originally manufactured for use as part of a gas range.

ENAMELING: *Principles and Practice*

It is the author's desire that more artists, craftsmen, and hobbyists should know how to make enamels, but it is not his desire that the precious beauties of the medium be misused or destroyed only in order to realize a quick monetary return for a small initial investment.

No enameler, and especially those whose names appear in the list of contemporary American enamelists in this book, has made his reputation on the number of small commercial pieces sold through department stores and shops alone His reputation has been made by realizing that he has within his grasp the knowledge and techniques which will allow him to produce a serious work of art. Unless he continually develops his sense of color, design, motifs, techniques and glazes, he is tempted to lose track of the finer ideals which he had as a student.

If one is seriously considering enameling as a livelihood, he will find it necessary to first equip his studio for quantity production. The suggestions which follow are of a practical nature and have been culled from some of my friends and former students who have developed enameling as a trade.

For production on a larger scale it is presupposed that the craftsman owns or has access to a large kiln. For the private studio, a kiln with an inside floor space of twelve to fifteen inches square should be adequate. As work progresses a second kiln of the same size could be purchased, but only if an assistant is employed and a great deal of firing is necessary.

With the interior space 12" × 12" × 6" it is possible to place four five-inch trays or bowls in the kiln at the same time, or one seven-inch and three four-inch bowls, or five four-inch trays. *Fig.* 114 shows a method of stacking for multiple firing. As the front of the kiln is cooled off in the process of stacking, the entire platform is removed after approximately two minutes, according to the type of glazes used, and turned before replacing in the kiln in order to mature all enamels at the same time.

The spray gun for tragacanth is essential and is used to replace the small atomizer mentioned in Chapter III. For dusting larger quantities of enamel one may improvise cylinders of tin cut from large tin cans with various meshes of wire screening soldered to one end.

Experiments, Suggestions for New Uses of Enamel

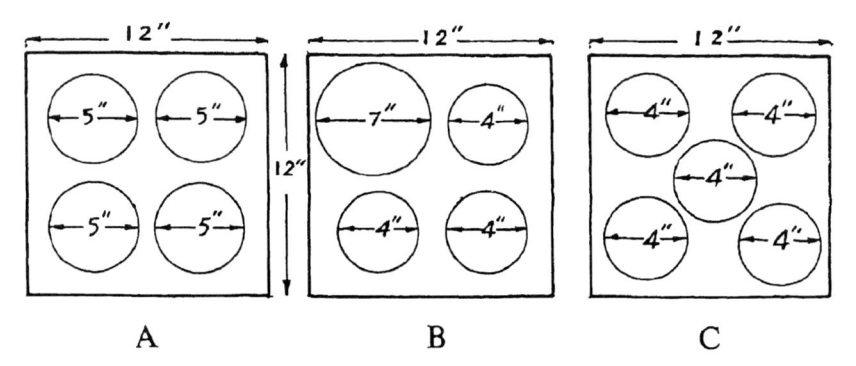

Fig. 114 In a kiln with a floor space 12 inches by 12 inches you can fire at one time: A Four 5-inch trays B. One 7-inch and three 4-inch trays or five 4-inch trays.

Designs must be simple, but effective (*Fig.* 115). Any of the techniques such as sgraffito, stenciling, crackling, metallic luster, or silver foil paillons are easily adaptable to quantity production. The slower process of inlaying each color by hand will probably be abandoned.

Stunning effects by overfiring can sometimes be controlled, but as a rule are too unpredictable for exact duplications. Perfect, smooth enameling, neat, clean edges, and a professional appearance must be obtained in the simplest and most expedient manner as the cost of each piece is regulated by the cost of labor per hour

Packing, shipping and bookkeeping enter into the picture and will usurp the time of the creative artist until he finds his own methods. It is well to remember when packing such pieces as trays, plates and bowls that the risk of sliding sideways in the box is always greater than that of pressure from above or below. If adequate crushed newspaper or excelsior is tightly packed at the side of the box breakage is considerably minimized.

The outlets for handling enamels are many and, at the time of this writing, there is a growing demand by art galleries, dealers, art shops, craft guilds, department stores, and smaller gift shops. The enamelist should decide what segment of the public will be interested in his particular type of enameling and then transact business with the stores where he thinks he will reach that clientele No artist can successfully produce in quantity all types of

ENAMELING: *Principles and Practice*

Fig. 115 Group of Enameled Objects, KENNETH F. BATES, 1950. These show the use of simple design motifs.

work and, by the same token, all types of buyers will not want his particular style of merchandise. Until he has found the proper outlet which allows him an appreciable return for his time and efforts, he cannot set up his program for work.

The most happily adjusted craftsmen I know who maintain individual businesses are those whose program for work is resolutely planned along a given number of work hours each week. These craftsmen are able to realize a certain profit per

Experiments, Suggestions for New Uses of Enamel

week and budget their business accordingly. Some shops or stores take work on consignment in which case the enamelist is expected to present a variety of designs which can be duplicated and also a few larger unique pieces. Other shops may start in this manner and eventually buy the pieces outright from the artist. All stores, galleries, and small shops take a commission ranging from twenty-five to fifty per cent. With larger department stores a mark-up of one hundred per cent is common practice.

A very satisfactory income is a plausible aim for an enamelist during his first year. Such an income presupposes that he has established the proper business outlets He may supplement this with sales made at ceramic exhibitions where a slightly smaller commission is taken by the galleries. He also may compete for any of several national prizes ranging from twenty-five to one hundred dollars. What happens to his income, his progress, or his reputation from this point on depends entirely on his own resourcefulness.

In conclusion, allow me to stress the fact that enameling is as modern as it is ancient Historians have written volumes concerning the heritage of enamels, but the present-day student should remember that the surface has hardly been scratched. By your original thinking and venturesome experimentation in the field of enameling you, also, may be creating history.

ENAMELING: *Principles and Practice*

CONTEMPORARY AMERICAN ENAMELISTS

A. ARTHUR AMES, Claremont, California. The enamel plate *Side Show*, 1950 by Mr. Ames is a skillful use of mixing the technique of sgraffito, dusting, and the spatula method.

Contemporary Enamelists

B JEAN AMES, Claremont, California. Mrs. Ames's compositions are lively and colorful.

ENAMELING: *Principles and Practice*

C. VIRGIL CANTINI, Pittsburgh, Pennsylvania. Mr. Cantini's work is outstanding for its boldness and simplicity

D. KARL DRERUP, Campton, New Hampshire. Mr. Drerup insists upon the highest standards in his work, both aesthetically and technically. The Metropolitan Museum of Art owns two of his pieces. (*Courtesy Metropolitan Museum of Art*)

E. WILLIAM DEHART, Albuquerque, New Mexico Mr. DeHart enamels almost entirely on sterling silver. His concave enameled disks strung on a leather thong make a charming necklace.

F. DORIS HALL, East Gloucester, Massachusetts. The sgraffito method was used almost entirely to produce this handsome nine-paneled mural, *Andante in Blue*, 1950. (*Courtesy Cleveland Museum of Art*)

Contemporary Enamelists

G. CHARLES BARTLEY JEFFERY, Cleveland, Ohio. Rich and colorful circular plaques with enamel over metal foil make up this ambitious ecclesiastical piece *Altar Cross*, 1942, which is typical of Mr. Jeffery's work. (*Courtesy Cleveland Museum of Art*)

ENAMELING: *Principles and Practice*

H. MIZI OTTEN, New York City, New York. Decorative figures and animals represent only a small portion of the work of this well-known enamelist of Viennese background.

I. LISEL SALZER, Livermore, California. Portraits are rare in enameling. Lisel Salzer attains technical mastery, likeness and charm in hers

Contemporary Enamelists

J. HAROLD TISHLER, Long Island, New York. Mr. Tishler has long been familiar with the technique, and has a perfect understanding of the medium of enameling in order to produce these easily salable objects.

K. MILDRED WATKINS, Cleveland, Ohio Miss Watkins' bracelet is an example of the rare and beautiful *basse-taille* technique of enameling. She is better known for her rich and deep-toned colors.

ENAMELING: *Principles and Practice*

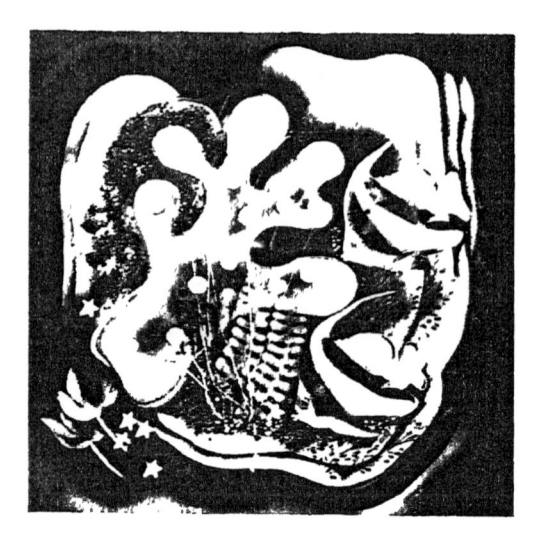

L. H EDWARD WINTER, Cleveland, Ohio. The use of steel plates upon which Mr Winter instigated the idea of enameled designs for exterior murals has built for him a national reputation. This plaque is called *Angel Fish*. (*Courtesy Metropolitan Museum of Art*).

M. ELLAMARIE AND JACKSON WOOLLEY, San Diego, California The sgraffito line with charm and character plus strong colors is typical of the work of Mr. and Mrs. Woolley.

APPENDIX

MATERIALS FOR ENAMELING AND WHERE TO BUY THEM

Enamels

B. K. Drakenfield and Co, 45 Park Place, New York 7, New York

Carpenter and Wood, Inc., Providence, Rhode Island

Ferro Enamel Corp., 4150 East 56 Street, Cleveland, Ohio

Harshaw Chemical Co., 1945 East 97 Street, Cleveland, Ohio

Maas and Waldstein Co., 440 Riverside Avenue, Newark 4, New Jersey

Metal Crafts Supply Co., Providence, Rhode Island

The O. Hommel Co., 209-213 Fourth Avenue, Pittsburgh 30, Pennsylvania

Thomas C. Thompson, 1205 Deerfield Road, Highland Park, Illinois

Wengers, Ltd., Etruria, Stokes-on-Trent, England

Kilns

Anchor Tool and Supply Co., 12 John Street, New York, New York

Brodhead-Garrett Co., Cleveland, Ohio

Electric Hotpack Co., Coltman Avenue and Melrose Street, Philadelphia, Pennsylvania

Hevi-Duty Electric Co., Milwaukee 1, Wisconsin

Peremy Equipment Co., Dept. 9, 893 Chambers Road, Columbus 8, Ohio

Metal Foils

Hastings and Co., 2314 Market Street, Philadelphia 3, Pennsylvania

Metallic Lusters

D. M. Campana Art Co., 442 North Wells Street, Chicago 10, Illinois

ENAMELING: *Principles and Practice*

Hanovia Chemical and Mfg Co., Chestnut Street and N. J. R. R Avenue, Newark, New Jersey

Harshaw Chemical Co , 1945 East 97 Street, Cleveland, Ohio

The O Hommel Co., 209-213 Fourth Avenue, Pittsburgh 30, Pennsylvania

CONTEMPORARY AMERICAN ENAMELISTS

Arthur Ames, 4094 Olive Hill Drive, Claremont, California

Jean Goodwin Ames (Mrs. Arthur Ames), 4094 Olive Hill Drive, Claremont, California

F. Carlton Ball, Mills College, Oakland 13, California

Kenneth F Bates, 7 East 194 Street, Euclid 19, Ohio

Kathe Berl, 1947 Broadway, New York 23, New York

J. Anthony Buzzelli, 400 West 57 Street, New York 19, New York

Virgil D. Cantini, 205 South Craig Street, Pittsburgh 13, Pennsylvania

Price Albert Chamberlin, 7022 Zoeter Avenue, Cleveland 3, Ohio

William DeHart, 215 North Rodey Street, Albuquerque, New Mexico

Karl Drerup, R F D. #1, Campton, New Hampshire

Marguerita O. Gillette, 7602 South Western Blvd., Dallas, Texas

Doris Hall (Mrs. Kalman Kubinyi), Rocky Neck Avenue, East Gloucester, Massachusetts

Maurice A. Heaton, West Nyack, New York

Mabel A. Hewit, 4714 Krueger Avenue, Cleveland, Ohio

Nancy Zerviah Hudson, 73 Mentor Avenue, Painesville, Ohio

Charles Bartley Jeffery, 1865 Nela Avenue, East Cleveland 12, Ohio

Robert T. King, Box 37, Alfred, New York

Kalman Kubinyi, Rocky Neck Avenue, East Gloucester, Massachusetts

Michael Natko, R.F.D. #3 Auburn Road, Chardon, Ohio

Jo Natko (Mrs. Michael Natko), R.F.D. #3 Auburn Road, Chardon, Ohio

J. M. Ney Co., Hartford, Connecticut

Mizi Otten, 160 Claremont Avenue, New York, New York

John Puskas, 1980 East 73 Street, Cleveland, Ohio

Appendix

Ruth Raemisch (Mrs.), 52 Boylston Avenue, Providence 6, Rhode Island
Arpad Rosti, 335 East 21 Street, New York 10, New York
Lisel Salzer, 1541 Pine Street, Livermore, California
Paul Schwarzkopf, Box 171, Fox River Grove, Illinois
Harold Tishler, 71 Sheriff Street, New York 2, New York
Anthony Vaiksnoras, 3675 East 140 Street, East Cleveland, Ohio
Mildred Watkins, 2109 Cornell Road, Cleveland 6, Ohio
Kay Whitcomb, Room 2-A, 1 Mt Vernon Street, Winchester, Massachusetts
H. Edward Winter, 11020 Magnolia Drive, Cleveland 6, Ohio
Jade Snow Wong, 1329 Powell Street, San Francisco 11, California
Ellamarie Woolley (Mrs Jackson Woolley), 969 Albion Street, San Diego 6, California
Jackson Woolley, 969 Albion Street, San Diego 6, California
Carl Wyman, 3630 Chelton Road, Cleveland 20, Ohio
Claire Witt Wyman, 3630 Chelton Road, Cleveland 20, Ohio

ENAMELING: *Principles and Practice*

TABLES OF INFORMATION USEFUL TO THE ENAMELIST

Apothecaries' Measure

8 fluid drams = 1 fluid ounce
16 fluid ounces = 1 pint
8 pints = 1 gallon

Apothecaries' Weight

20 grains = 1 scruple
3 scruples = 1 dram
8 drams = 1 ounce
12 ounces = 1 pound

Avoirdupois Weight

27⅓ grains = 1 dram
16 drams = 1 ounce
16 ounces = 1 pound

Troy Weight

24 grains = 1 pennyweight
20 pennyweights = 1 ounce
12 ounces = 1 pound

Appendix
CIRCUMFERENCE AND AREA OF CIRCLE

AREA (in sq. inches)	DIAMETER (in inches)	CIRCUMFERENCE (in inches)
05	¼	.78
20	½	1.57
.44	¾	2.35
.79	1	3.14
1.23	1¼	3.92
1 77	1½	4.71
2.41	1¾	5.49
3.14	2	6.28
3.98	2¼	7.07
4.91	2½	7.85
5.94	2¾	8.64
7.07	3	9.43
8.30	3¼	10.21
9 62	3½	11.00
11.04	3¾	11.78
12.57	4	12.57
14.19	4¼	13.35
15.90	4½	14.14
17.72	4¾	14.92
19.63	5	15.71
21.65	5¼	16.49
23 76	5½	17.28
25 97	5¾	18.06
28.27	6	18.85
30.68	6¼	19.63
33.18	6½	20.42
35.78	6¾	21.21
38.48	7	21.99
41.28	7¼	22.78
44.18	7½	23.56
47.17	7¾	24.35
50.27	8	25.13
53.46	8¼	25.92

ENAMELING: *Principles and Practice*

AREA (in sq. inches)	DIAMETER (in inches)	CIRCUMFERENCE (in inches)
56.76	8½	26.70
60.13	8¾	27.49
63 62	9	28.27
67 20	9¼	29.06
70.88	9½	29.85
74.66	9¾	30.63
78.54	10	31.42
95 03	11	34.56
113.10	12	37.70
132.73	13	40.84
153 94	14	43 98
176.72	15	47.12
201.06	16	50.27
226.98	17	53.41
254 47	18	56 55
283.53	19	59 69
314 16	20	62.83

TABLE OF MELTING POINTS

	DEGREES Fahrenheit	DEGREES Centigrade
Lead	621	327
Bronze (Copper 80%, Tin 20%)	1868	1020
Gold 24K	1945	1063
Gold 18K	1700	927
Gilding Metal (Copper 95%, Zinc 5%)	1950	1065
Copper	1981	1083
Platinum	3191	1755
Fine Silver	1761	960
Sterling Silver (Silver 92.5%, Copper 7.5%)	1640	898
Tin	450	232
Zinc	787	419

Appendix

CONVERSION OF CERAMIC FIRING CONES

CONE	DEGREES *Centigrade*	DEGREES *Fahrenheit*
021	595	1103
020	625	1157
019	630	1166
018	670	1238
017	720	1328
016	735	1357
015	770	1418
014	795	1463
013	825	1517
012	840	1544
011	875	1607
010	890	1634
09	930	1706
08	945	1733
07	975	1787
06	1005	1841
05	1030	1886
04	1050	1922
03	1080	1976
02	1095	2003

CONVERSION OF B. & S. GAUGE INTO INCHES

THICKNESS (*in inches*)	BROWN & SHARPE (*B. & S.*) *Gauge*
.289	1
.258	2
.229	3
.206	4
.181	5
.162	6
.144	7
.128	8

ENAMELING: *Principles and Practice*

THICKNESS (in inches)	BROWN & SHARPE (B. & S) Gauge
.114	9
.101	10
090	11
.080	12
.072	13
.064	14
057	15
.050	16
.045	17
040	18
.036	19
.032	20
028	21
.025	22
.023	23
.020	24
.018	25
.015	26
.014	27
.013	28
.011	29
.010	30
.009	31
.007	32
.007	33
.006	34
.006	35

TABLE SHOWING WEIGHT OF COPPER PER SQUARE FOOT

POUNDS	B. & S. GAUGE
7.19	6
6.40	7
5.70	8

Appendix

POUNDS	B. & S. GAUGE
5.07	9
4.52	10
4.02	11
3.50	12
3.19	13
3.84	14
2.53	15
2.25	16
2.00	17
1.79	18
1.59	19
1.41	20
1.26	21
1.13	22
1.00	23
.89	24
.79	25
.71	26
.44	30

TABLE SHOWING WEIGHT OF STERLING SILVER PER SQUARE INCH

TROY OUNCES	B. & S. GAUGE
.443	12
.351	14
.278	16
.221	18
.175	20
.139	22
.110	24
.087	26

ENAMELING: *Principles and Practice*

WHERE TO FIND INFORMATION ON HOW TO COLOR COPPER

American Machinists' Handbook, McGraw-Hill Book Co, Inc, New York, New York, c1945

The Brown & Sharpe Handbook, Brown & Sharpe Mfg. Co., Providence, Rhode Island

Herculoy, Revere Copper & Brass, Inc., New York, New York, c1937

Metal Art Crafts, by John G Miller, D. Van Nostrand, Inc., New York, New York, c1948

Metal Coloring and Bronzing, by Arthur H Hiorm, Macmillan and Co, London, c1929

Modern Metalcraft, by John L Feirer, The Manual Arts Press, Illinois, c1946

The Starrett Book for Student Machinists, The L. S. Starrett Co, Athol, Massachusetts, c1941

GLOSSARY

Anneal To soften metals by heating to a pink color.

Basse-taille. A type of enameling making use of transparent enamels fired over a carved or chased metal surface

Bright dip A solution of equal parts sulfuric acid and nitric acid plus a few grains of salt, used for final cleaning of copper.

Burnisher. A blunt agate or metal tool for smoothing metal or metal foil.

Champlevé A type of enameling making use of transparent or opaque enamels fired into etched or carved areas, leaving the metal partly exposed.

Cloisonné. A type of enameling in which each color is separated by thin metal ribbons, or wires.

Counterenamel Enamel used on the reverse side of a piece to relieve the tension of the expansion and contraction of the enamel on the right side

En résille A type of enameling making use of finely ground colors fired into small depressions in crystal.

Flux. A clear enamel with no oxide of metal for coloring.

Frit. A term given to enamel while still in the ground, or chunk, state.

Glass brush. A group of glass fibers tied together with cord, used to polish or brighten dull metal surfaces.

Grisaille. A type of enameling made by firing various thicknesses of white opaque enamel on a black opaque background.

Gum tragacanth. A gum from Asiatic trees which is applied in a water solution as a binder for enamels.

Hard enamel. An enamel which fuses at a high temperature and is usually impervious to acid.

High-fire enamel. An enamel which becomes molten at 1600° F. or a higher temperature.

Kiln An electric or gas muffled furnace used for firing enamels.

ENAMELING: *Principles and Practice*

Limoges enamel A type of enameling having originated in Limoges, France, which makes use of juxtaposed colors covering the entire surface of the metal.

Low-fire enamel An enamel which becomes molten at any temperature below 1250° F.

Mesh The coarseness or fineness of a screen which is designated by the number of openings per square inch caused by the crossing of threads

Mushroom anvil. A steel form with a mushroomlike appearance used in shaping metal bowls.

Oil of lavender. An oil used in overglaze painting as a spreader but which burns away in the firing process

Opalescent enamels. Enamels having a milky iridescence when fired. They are seldom used by present-day enamelists.

Opaque enamels Enamels which cover the metal densely when brought to the fusing point.

Overglaze colors Finely ground enamels used in making painted enamels.

Oxidation. Discoloration of metal caused by oxygen.

Paillons Small pieces of metal foil over which transparent enamels are fired.

Planishing. A light hammering for toughening and finishing metal.

Plique-à-jour A type of enameling making use of transparent enamels suspended in small openings of metal, giving the appearance of stained-glass windows.

Pyrometer. A gauge for measuring temperature in the kiln.

Resist. Any medium used in the etching process to protect certain areas of metal from the action of the acid.

Rheostat An arrangement for controlling the temperature of the electric kiln by means of variable resistance

Scriber A sharp-pointed steel instrument used for engraving or tracing lines on metal.

Sgraffito. A technique in enameling whereby a linear motif is produced by scratching through one enamel revealing a different colored ground.

Soft enamel. An enamel which fuses at a low temperature and is easily affected by acid

Glossary

Squeegee oil. A thick, sticky oil used in silk-screen printing which can be mixed with overglaze enamels as a binder It disappears in the firing process.

Stilts. Various pieces of high-fired clay for holding enameled objects in the kiln

Stoning Leveling the surface of enamels by grinding with a Carborundum stone.

Stylus. A dull-pointed instrument for tracing lines on paper or metal with the use of carbon paper

T stake. A steel form shaped like the letter T, used in shaping metal bowls, etc.

Translucent enamel A term used synonymously with transparent enamel

Transparent enamel. Enamel which allows the color of the metal to be seen through it when fused.

Tripoli A compound of tallow and various grades of abrasive sold in cake form for removing scratches from metal It is applied to the felt buffing wheel.

Vitrifiable color. Oxides of metal which are simply mixed with flux.

Vitrified color. Oxides of metal which have previously been melted or dissolved with flux.

BIBLIOGRAPHY

ADDISON, JULIA DEWOLF *Arts and Crafts in the Middle Ages,* L. C. Page & Co , Boston, c1908.

BROWN, W. N. *The Art of Enameling,* Scott, Greenwood & Co., London, c1900.

BOSSERT, H T *Geschichte des Kunstgewerbes* (Vol. I and Vol. V), Ernst Wasmuth, Berlin, c1928.

BURGER, WILLY *Abendlandische Schmelzarbeiten,* R. C Schmidt and Co , Berlin, c1930.

CLEVELAND MUSEUM OF ART. *Bulletin,* Number 9, November, 1926.

CUNYNGHAME, H. H *Art Enamelling on Metal,* Archibald Constable & Co. Ltd., Westminster, c1899.

DAVENPORT, CYRIL. *Jewellry,* Methuen & Co., London, c1905.

DAWSON, MRS NELSON. *Enamels (Little Books on Art Series),* A C. McClurg and Co., Chicago, Illinois, c1908.

DAWSON, NELSON. *Goldsmiths' and Silversmiths' Work,* G. P. Putnam's Sons, New York, c1907.

DAY, LEWIS F. *Enamelling,* B. T. Batsford, London, c1907.

DE KONINGH, H *The Preparation of Precious and Other Metal Work For Enamelling,* The Norman W Henley Publishing Co., New York, c1930

Encyclopaedia Britannica. "Enamel," Vol. 8.

FEIRER, JOHN L. *Modern Metalcraft,* The Manual Arts Press, Peoria, Illinois, c1946.

FISHER, ALEXANDER. *The Art of Enamelling Upon Metal,* The Studio, London, c1906.

HILDBURGH, W L *Medieval Spanish Enamels,* Oxford University Press, London, c1936.

LABARTE, JULES. *Peinture en Émail—Recherches sur La Peinture en Émail dans L'antiquité et au Moyen Age,* Victor Didron, Paris, c1856.

LAVEDAN, PIERRE. *Léonard Limosin et Les Émailleurs Française,* Henri Laurens, Paris.

Bibliography

LEHNERT, GEORG HERMANN. ed., *Illustrierte Geschichte des Kunstgewerbes* (Vol I), M. Oldenbourg, Berlin, c1907

MARTIN, CHARLES J. *How to Make Modern Jewelry,* Simon and Schuster, New York, c1949

MILLER, JOHN G *Metal Art Crafts,* D. Van Nostrand Co Inc., New York, c1948.

MILLIKEN, WILLIAM. *Early Enamels in Cleveland Museum of Art*— Connoiseur Oct. 126v.76

MORGAN, J. PIERPONT *Catalogue of the Collection of Jewels and Precious Works of Art,* Chiswick Press, London, c1910.

NEUBURGER, ALBERT *The Technical Arts and Science of the Ancients,* Macmillan Co , New York, c1930

PACK, GRETA *Jewelry and Enamelling,* D. Van Nostrand Co Inc., New York, c1941

PIJOÁN, JOSÉ. *Summa Artis* (Vol. VII and VIII) Espasa-Calpe, Madrid, c1931

ROGERS, FRANCES and BEARD, ALICE *5000 Years of Gems and Jewelry,* Frederick A. Stokes Co., New York, c1940

ROCHOWANSKI, L W. *Ein Führer Durch Das Osterreichische,* Verlag Heinz and Corp , Kunstgewerbe, Leipzig, c1930

ROSE, AUGUSTUS FOSTER, and CIRINO, A *Jewelry Making and Design,* Metalcrafts Publishing Co., Providence, Rhode Island, c1917.

ROSE, AUGUSTUS F. *Copper Work,* The Davis Press, Worcester, Massachusetts, c1906.

RUPIN, ERNEST *L'oeuvre de Limoges,* Alphonse Picard, Paris, c1890.

SMITH, H CLIFFORD. *Jewellry,* Methuen & Co., London, c1908.

TUCKER, ALLEN *Design and the Idea,* American Federation of Arts, c1939.

THOMPSON, THOMAS E *Enameling on Copper and Other Metals,* T. C. Thompson Co., c1950.

WHEATLEY, HENRY G. and DELAMOTTE, PHILIP H. *Art Work in Gold and Silver (Medieval),* Scribner and Welford, New York, c1882.

WIENER, LOUIS. *Hand Made Jewelry,* D. Van Nostrand Co., New York, c1948.

ZVENIGORODSKOÏ, A. V. *Histoire et Monuments des Émaux Byzantins,* Francfort sur Mein, par N. Kondakow, c1892 (Pierpont Morgan Collection).

INDEX

abstractions, 85
acid bath, 52-54, 63-64, 83, 128-129
air pockets, 100-101
Albert Museum, 23
alcohol, wood, 48
    denatured, 48
alkaline earths, 43
alkalizing, 54-56
American enameling, 37-38
ammonia, 54, 99
annealing, 49
antimony, 42, 89
anvil, mushroom, 45, 50
Argument in a Limoges Market Place, 105
Art of Enamelling on Metals, 36, 39
asbestos, 60, 61
Asia Minor, 24
Austrian Applied Arts, 37
Austrian Museum of Art and Industry, 37

backgrounds, 86, 90-91
backing enamel, 57-60, 119
backless enamel, 34, 131-132
barbaric enamel, 24, 125
basse-taille, 135-136, 140
Battersea, 33, 85
bezel, 93, 94, 96, 111, 124, 172
Bird of Paradise Flower, 67
Bird Watch, The, 108
blowtorch, 71-73, 81, 112, 161, 162-163, 174
    gas, 162
    mouth, 162
blowtorch method, 71-73
Bole, Mrs. Benjamin P., 119
borates, 42
borax, 41, 113, 115
bowls, 70
brass, 169-171
bright dip, 88
British Museum, 23
bronze, 29

Brunswick, 25
brush, glass, 79, 80, 112
buffers, 43
buffing, 117, 130
Bunsen burner, 71
burnishing, 78, 101, 104
Byzantine enamels, 23-25, 34, 42, 109

capillary attraction, 133-135, 173
carbon, 98-99
Carborundum stone, 55, 78, 88, 97, 116, 130
Cathedral of St. Blasius, 27
Caucasus, 24
Cellini, Benvenuto, 131
Celtic enamels, 22-23
champlevé enamel, 22, 23, 24, 28-29, 85, 92, 125-130, 140, 144, 173
    buffing, 130
    design for, 126-127
    enamels for, 129-130
    plating, 127
    polishing, 130
China painting, 92, 164
Chinese enamels, 34-36, 117, 163, 169
chipping, 57-58
Church of St. Sophia, 24
Cinerarias, 85
cleaning, 51-52
Cleveland Institute of Art, 120
Cleveland Museum of Art, 26-27, 38, 120, 138
cloisonné, 23, 24, 28-29, 34-36, 92, 97, 104, 109-124, 140, 144, 150
cloisons, 24, 139
Cluny Museum, 23
coatings, enamel, 99-101
cobalt oxide, 42
coloration method, 63-65
coloring, 74-82
colors, 42, 57, 81, 82
    characteristics of, 83-91
    depth in, 156
    design and, 141

Index

gas flame and, 162-163
vibration in, 145
vitrifiable, 164-166
vitrified, 164-166
Constantinople, 24
copper oxide, 42
Corundite, 45
counterenamel, 57-60, 63, 64, 75-76, 78, 86, 90, 93, 97-98, 113, 120, 173
cracking, 57-58, 81, 89, 90, 102, 104, 113
crystal, 139
rock, 139
Cunynghame, H. H., 36, 39n
cutch silver, 77

Danube, 24
deep bowls, 70
depth, 157
illusion, 97
design, 141-157
tracing, 63-64
transferring of, 98-99
Design and the Idea, 147
dial, 84, 168
dip, bright, 88
directionalism, 147-150
dividers, 50
dogwood mallet, 44, 49
drying, 59-60
dusting, 44, 57, 89, 166, 167, 172
dusting method, 68-69, 70

ecclesiastical enamels, 29, 155-156
edges, 144-147
Egypt, 24
Eilbertus, 28
elasticity, 41, 93
embossed line, 166-168
en résille, 138-140
enamel
abstract effects in, 85
air pockets in, 101
American, 37-38
application of, 114-115
background, 86, 90-91
backing, 57-60, 119
backless, 34, 131-132
barbaric, 24, 125
brass and, 169-171
Byzantine, 23-25, 34, 42, 109
Celtic, 22-23

champlevé, 22, 23, 24, 28-29, 85, 92, 125-130, 140, 144, 173
Chinese, 34-36, 117, 163, 169
cloisonné, 23, 24, 28-29, 34-36, 92, 97, 104, 109-124, 140, 144, 150
coatings, 99-101
colors in, 42, 57, 74-91
depth illusion in, 97, 156
design in, 63-64, 98-99, 141-157
directionalism in, 147-150
drying, 59-60
ecclesiastical, 29, 155-156
edges in, 144-147
elasticity, 41, 93
embossed lines in, 166-168
English, 24, 33, 36
equipment for, 176-177
experimentation in, 160-172
firing, 36, 40, 45-46, 60-63, 66, 67, 69, 71-73, 74-82, 76-89, 95, 97-100, 104, 115-116, 133-134, 144-147, 150, 163-164, 168, 169
French, 29, 34, 92, 135-140, 169
glass and, 73, 171-172
German, 25-29
Gothic, 125
grisaille, 101-102, 136-138, 140
handcraft in, 36
hardness of, 41, 81, 82, 83
inlaid, 65-67, 92, 145-147
Italian, 34, 131
Japanese, 34-36
jewels, 160-162
Limoges, 29, 36, 42, 77, 92-108, 137, 140, 174
livelihood in, 175-179
Merovingian, 24, 125
neutral tones in, 84
new uses for, 172-175
opalescent, 39, 40, 42
opaque, 29, 37, 39, 40, 42, 48, 56, 67, 75-76, 83-91, 144, 168, 169
overglaze, 39, 40, 102, 138, 164-166
panels, 111-112
portraiture, 30-32, 107-108
Roman, 23
Russian, 24, 33-34, 131
Saxon, 22
scale in, 143
sgraffito, 166, 168-169
shading in, 101-102, 169
soft, 41, 81-82, 83

205

ENAMELING: *Principles and Practice*

stencil method in, 69, 70, 147
stress in, 147-150
subject matter in, 150-156
tactility in, 31-32
textures of, 82, 100
thin line in, 166
transparent, 29, 39, 40, 42, 48, 57, 67, 74, 75-80, 145, 174
types of, 39-40
vibration in, 143-144
Viennese, 37
vitrifiable, 164-166
vitrified, 164-166
washing of, 56-57, 79-80, 97
wire, 34, 112-113
enameling tools, 47-48
English enamels, 24, 33, 36
equipment, 176-177
etching, 128-129
experimentation, 160-172

ferric chloride, 129
fire glaze, 62, 68, 88, 97, 112, 130, 163-164
firing, 36, 40, 45-46, 66, 67, 69, 71-73, 74-88, 95, 97-100, 104, 115-116, 133-134, 144-147, 150, 163-164, 168, 169
Fisher, Alexander, 36
flint glass, 42
flushing, 116
flux, 39, 42, 78, 79, 81, 88, 89, 90, 92, 97, 101, 113, 138, 147, 164, 168
Francis I, 32
French enamels, 29, 34, 92, 135-140, 169
frit, 40, 42, 109, 161
Fruits of My Orchard, 104
fusibility, 150
fusing, 71, 83, 132

Gallerie d'Apollon, 139
gas flame colorations, 162-163
German enamels, 25-29
Gertrudis I, Countess, 27
gilding, 28, 89
glass, enamel and, 73, 171-172
  flint, 42
  paste, 139
glass brush, 79, 80, 112
gold, 75, 76-78, 89, 95, 99, 100, 101, 103, 109, 111-112, 113, 115, 123

cleaning of, 112
gold oxide, 42, 87-88
Golden Gate International Exposition, 38
Gothic enamel, 125
grisaille, 101-102, 136-138, 140
Guelph, 26
gum tragacanth, 44, 48, 55, 58, 59 69, 71, 78, 118, 119, 121, 123, 134, 161, 168-169

halation, 91, 105
handcraft, 36
hard dial, 84, 168
hard enamel, 41, 81, 82, 83
heating, colors in, 62
Henry the Lion, Duke, 27
hydrochloric acid, 88

Inception of Spring, 106
inlaid method, 65-67, 92, 145-147
iridium oxide, 42
iron oxide, 41, 42, 72
isopropyl, 48
Italian enamel, 34, 131

Jansen, Stephan Theodore, 33
Japanese enamels, 34-36
jeweler's rouge, 43
jeweler's scribe, 47, 63, 128
jewels, enameled, 160-162

kiln, 44, 45-47, 59, 60-63, 73, 74
  electric, 71

lavender, oil of, 40, 102, 103, 165
Lea Buffing Compound, 55
lead oxide, 41, 42
lime, 41, 43
Limoges enamel, 29, 36, 42, 77, 92-108, 137, 140, 174
Limousin, Léonard, 30-31, 32, 107
Louis XIV, 32
Louvre, 23, 139
lusters, 102-104
LW-10, 45

magnesia, 41, 43
mallet, dogwood, 44, 49
  rawhide, 44, 49
manganese oxide, 89
melting, test for, 81-82

206

Index

Merovingian enamel, 24, 125
mesh, 40, 42, 43, 68, 97, 114, 115, 129, 167, 170, 173
metal foils, 75-77, 78
metallic paint, 79, 102-104
Metropolitan Museum, 24
Meuse, 25
mica, 95, 173
Milliken, Dr, 138
Morgan, J. Pierpont, Collection, 24, 139
Mosgo, Charles, 160-161
Moussorgsky, Modest Petrovitch, 105
mushroom anvil, 45, 50

"Nardon," 29, 92
National Ceramic Exhibition, 37
National Naval Medical Center, 131
neutral tones, 84
Nicrome, 47
nitric acid, 52, 79, 88, 128-129
nonobjective approach, 150-152

oil of lavender, 40, 102, 103, 165
oil of sassafras, 40, 123, 165
Onondaga Potteries, 38
opalescent enamel, 39, 40, 42
opaque enamel, 29, 37, 39, 40, 42, 48, 56, 67, 75-76, 83-91, 144, 168, 169
Otto II, 25
Otto IV, 27
overfiring, 76, 82, 90, 144-147
overglaze enamel, 39, 40, 102, 138, 164-166
overpainting, 129, 164-166
oxidation, 54-56, 80, 85, 109, 145, 174
oxides, 40
  cobalt, 42
  copper, 42
  gold, 42, 87-88
  iridium, 42
  iron, 41, 42, 72
  lead, 41, 42
  manganese, 42, 89
  platinum, 42
  tin, 42

paillons, 77, 78, 82, 89, 100-101, 177
Pagan Sacrifice, A, 137
Pala d'Oro, 24
palette, 82, 84
palette knife, 40

panels, 111-112
paraffin, 127
Penicaud II, 29, 92
Penicaud, Jean, 29, 92
Penicaud, Léonard, 29, 36
Persia, 24
pickling, 79, 88, 112, 113
Pictures from an Exhibition, 105
planishing hammer, 45, 49
platinum oxide, 42
plique-à-jour, 34, 131-135, 140, 172-173
  by capillary attraction, 133-134
  on copper plate, 132
  on mica, 132-133
Poilleué, Jean, 137
pointer, 43, 47, 64, 65, 76, 97, 114, 169
polishing, 130
Portrait of a Lady, 107
portraiture, in enamels, 30-32, 107-108
potash, 41
pyrometer, 62

rawhide, mallet, 44, 49
Reformation, 27
refractory stilts, 65
Renaissance, 34, 36
resists, 128
Reymond, Pierre, 30
rheostat, 63
Rhine, 25
Robineau, Adelaide Alsop, 37
Rochowanski, L. W., 37
rock crystal, 139
Roman enamel, 23
Russian enamels, 24, 33-34, 131

sable brushes, 44
St Mark's Cathedral, 24
salt, 88
sand, 41
sassafras, oil of, 40, 123, 165
Saxon enamels, 22-23
Saxony, 25
scale, 143
scriber, 85, 99
Second Crusade, 27
sgraffito, 166, 168-169
shading, 101-102, 164-165
sifting method, 68-71
silica, 41

207

ENAMELING: *Principles and Practice*

silicates, 42
silver, 76-78, 79-81, 82, 89, 90, 100-101, 109, 123
 best color for, 80
silver powder, 104
slag, 41
sludge, 97
soda, 41, 115
sodium uranate, 90
soft enamel, 41, 81-82, 83
"soft for silver," 84
soldering, 95-96, 113, 117-119, 174
South Kensington Museum, 139
spatula, 43, 47, 61, 76, 78, 97, 102, 120, 168
spatula method, 65-67, 69, 89
spreader, 43, 47-48, 65, 115, 120, 168
squeegee oil, 40, 102, 123, 165, 166
Stabler, Harold, 36
stake tree, 45, 49
stands for firing, 65
stencil process, 69, 70, 147
stilts, 43
 refractory, 65
stilts and stands for firing, 65
stoning, 36, 116-117, 123
Strelitzia, 70
stress, 147-150
stylus, 98
subject matter, 150-156
sulfuric acid, 79, 88
Syracuse Museum of Fine Arts, 37-38

T stake, 45, 50
tactility, 31-32
Taft Museum, 31
texture, 82, 100
Theophano, 25

thin line, 166
three-dimensional effects, 136-138
tin, 89
tin oxide, 42
Tombac, 89
tracing, 63-65
tragacanth (*see* gum tragacanth)
transferring design, 98-99
translucent enamel (*see* transparent enamel)
transparent enamel, 29, 39, 40, 42, 48, 57, 67, 74, 75-80, 145, 174
transparent tests, 78-80
trimming, 50
tripoli, 43, 117, 130
Tucker, Allen, 147
turpentine, 40

uranium, 42, 90

Venice, 24
vibration, 143-144
Vienna School of Arts and Crafts, 37
Viennese enamel, 37
Victoria Museum, 23
vitrifiable color, 164-166
vitrified color, 164-166
volatile oil, 40, 73

warping, 71, 94
washing, 56-57, 79-80, 97
Wedgwood, 168
wire, 112-113
wire enamel, 34
wood alcohol, 48

zinc, 89